The Forgotten Books of the Bible

The Forgotten Books of the Bible

Recovering the Five Scrolls for Today

Robert Williamson Jr.

Fortress Press
Minneapolis

THE FORGOTTEN BOOKS OF THE BIBLE
Recovering the Five Scrolls for Today

Common English Bible ©2011. Used by permission. All rights reserved.

Cover image: Wikimedia Commons: Song of songs by Gustave Moreau (1826–1898)
Cover design: Paul Soupiset

Print ISBN: 978-1-5064-0626-8
eBook ISBN: 978-1-5064-0627-5

The paper used in this publication meets the minimum requirements of American National Standard for Information Sciences — Permanence of Paper for Printed Library Materials, ANSI Z329.48-1984.

Manufactured in the U.S.A.

For Lindy,
Anna Kate,
Siduri,
and
Ruthie,
who bring so much joy to life

Contents

Acknowledgments

My interest in the "forgotten" books of the Bible began years ago when I was a student at Columbia Theological Seminary in Atlanta. There, Walter Brueggemann taught us to view the Bible as a collection of competing testimonies about God. In characteristic fashion, he insisted we pay attention to the biblical "counter-testimonies" (his word) that trouble the more settled theological claims of the majority tradition. I was hooked.

It was Kathleen O'Connor who first showed me the beauty of Lamentations, which she read as an act of witness on behalf of those who suffer. I became intrigued by the possibilities that marginal books like Lamentations might hold for people at the margins of faith—those who suffer, those who doubt, those who protest. In my graduate work at Emory University, I shifted my attention to Ecclesiastes with my teachers Carol Newsom and Brent Strawn. There I discovered a biblical witness for those who are disillusioned and overwhelmed by the futility of life. Along the way, I studied Song of Songs with David Blumenthal, delving into its sensuous poetry and its embrace of human sexuality. My first lectures as a graduate instructor were on Lamentations and Song of Songs in courses taught by John Hayes and David Petersen.

This book itself started to take shape several years ago when I was invited to deliver the Spring Lectures at the Kirk in the Pines in Hot Springs Village, Arkansas. Since then, I've developed my ideas in lectures at Temple B'nai Israel and Second Presbyterian Church in Little Rock, Arkansas, as well as First Presbyterian Church in Conway, Arkansas. I've also learned a great deal studying these texts with my students at Hendrix College, particularly in my "Skeptics in Scripture" and "Race, Gender, Empire, & the Bible" courses.

I'm especially grateful to my student Laura-Beth Durham and to the Reverend Marie Mainard O'Connell, whose work on the Song of Songs has informed my own. My friends Donny Underwood and Fred McLean graciously allowed me to share a story of their lives in the introduction.

As anyone who has ever written anything can attest—writing is hard. For me, at least, it wouldn't be possible without a support network of friends and loved ones offering insight and encouragement. I'm grateful to my parents, Bob and Eva Williamson, who raised me in a family where the Bible was always part of the conversation and in a church where God was all love and grace. My friends at Mercy Community Church of Little Rock have made me a more sensitive reader of biblical texts—and a better human being more generally. My friend Amy Robertson, a brilliant Hebrew Bible scholar who serves as executive director of Congregation Bet Haverim in Atlanta, read early drafts of this book and helped me find my voice. My friends and colleagues Anne Apple, Colin Bagby, and Miranda Donakey also provided invaluable feedback.

The vast majority of this book was written at the Kavanaugh Starbucks in Little Rock, Arkansas. My thanks to Gabe and all the baristas for keeping me well-caffeinated and for allowing me to occupy a table for what was probably an unreasonable number of hours. I'm also grateful to the musical artists who provided the soundtrack for my writing. I would tell you who they were, but I'm a little afraid you might judge me for some of my musical choices. Let's just say I'm never ever ever going to tell you. Like ever.

I'm especially grateful to everyone at Fortress Press for helping make this book a reality. Tony Jones first saw the possibilities for this project and brought me on board with Fortress Press. My editor, Lisa Kloskin, read the initial draft with great care, giving incisive comments and encouragement that improved the final manuscript considerably. Layne Johnson, Katie Clifford, and Allyce Amidon shepherded the book through production and marketing. I couldn't have hoped for a better team.

Finally, my unending gratitude to my beloved, Lindy Vogado, without whose support and encouragement this book wouldn't have been possible. I'm blessed to have a partner who not only makes space in our marriage for my writing but who also reads and comments on drafts with keen theological and pastoral insights. What's more, while I was bringing this book into the world, Lindy was giving life to our daughter, Anna Kate, who (at the time of this writing) will be born any day now. As long as I live, I will never accomplish anything so amazing.

This book is dedicated to Lindy and to Anna Kate—along with our dogs Siduri and Ruth Bader Ginsbark. It's a joy to share a life with you.

Robert Williamson Jr.
October 31, 2017
The Five Hundredth Anniversary of the Reformation

Introduction

The most beautiful lesson I have ever learned about the Bible was taught to me by a gay homeless couple struggling to survive on the streets of Little Rock, Arkansas, where I live.[1] Mind you, I'm an ordained minister and a biblical studies professor with a PhD, so I have learned a *lot* of lessons about the Bible. I have also taught a lot of lessons about the Bible myself. But none as beautiful as this one.

The text was the book of Ruth, and the context was a marriage proposal. These two men had been together for nearly a decade, though they hadn't been homeless at first. They had ended up living on the streets when Donny, one partner in the couple, had been shot in the face, damaging part of his frontal lobe. The injury meant that he could no longer hold a job or even function well in society, as he had suffered a loss of impulse control and was in a great deal of constant pain. So Donny moved to the streets.

His partner, Fred, still had an apartment and a steady job, but he couldn't bear the thought of Donny living on the streets all alone. So he gave up his apartment, quit his job, and became homeless so he could support the man that he loved.

On the day of the marriage proposal, some five or six years later, Donny expressed his love for Fred by relating their story to that of the biblical character Ruth, who had likewise given up her life to support her mother-in-law, Naomi, in her time of greatest need. Donny wept as he recited Ruth's words of commitment to Naomi, used so often in wedding services but never with such profound resonance:

> Wherever you go, I will go;
> and where you stay, I will stay.
> Your people will be my people,
> and your God will be my God.
> Wherever you die, I will die,
> and there I will be buried. (Ruth 1:16–17)[2]

I had never understood the profundity of Ruth until that moment. I had never known what it meant to truly give up your life to love someone else.

The wedding proposal took place during a service at a little church I founded a few years back called Mercy Community Church of Little Rock. We are a tiny, multidenominational community with no money and no building of our own—but we have a lot of love. Mercy Community Church welcomes people from all walks of life, but most of our community is living on the streets or in shelters.

I confess I was a little nervous when Donny told me he was going to propose to Fred during the time when we offer gifts of ourselves to the community. Honestly, I wasn't entirely sure what my little homeless community thought about gay marriage, and I wasn't sure how they would handle the proposal. But the scene that unfolded was astounding to behold. The community erupted into applause. The guitar player started strumming the chords to Donny's favorite song, "I'll Fly Away." People grabbed drums and tambourines as the community burst into song. They started dancing and shouting and hugging each other. It never occurred to anyone to be anything but happy for Donny and Fred, who had found a love like that of Ruth and Naomi.

I should have known better than to be nervous about my community. We founded Mercy Community Church because we believe the liberation teaching that God is more active in the margins of society than at its center. We created a community that tries to decenter the center in order to receive the wisdom of those who have been treated as outsiders, pushed to the edges, and forgotten. When we take the time to listen, those forgotten voices can teach us profound things.

The Bible, too, contains forgotten voices. Indeed, it contains whole books that have been marginalized in the life of the church, pushed to the edges by the great scriptures like Genesis and Isaiah and the Gospels. The commitment of this book is that those forgotten books of the Bible have profound things to teach us, too.

When I speak of the "forgotten books of the Bible," I have a particular set of texts in mind: Song of Songs, Ruth, Lamentations, Ecclesiastes, and Esther. These five books have never had an easy time of it. Even centuries ago when the Jewish rabbis were deciding what books were to be considered holy, several of these books barely made the cut. Song of Songs and Ecclesiastes were most disputed—the former because it was too sexy and the latter because it was too depressing. The book of Esther was suspect because it never even mentions God.

Yet in the end, the Jewish tradition not only declared all of these books holy but ultimately elevated them to a special status in the tradition. The five books together became known as the *Chamesh Megillot*—the Five Scrolls—and they were each assigned to be read in association with a particular Jewish holiday. The Song of Songs is read on Passover, Ruth as part of the Feast of Weeks (Shavuot). Lamentations commemorates the destruction of the temple on Tisha B'Av. Ecclesiastes is read during the Feast of Booths (Sukkot) and Esther in the celebration of Purim. Once nearly marginalized by the Jewish tradition, these books now have a central place in the life of that community.

Not so in the Christian church. While the Christian tradition also affirms the holiness of these books as part of the Christian Old Testament, they hardly ever make an appearance in the actual life of the church—or in the lives of most Christians. Occasionally we might read Ruth's pledge to Naomi (Ruth 1:16–17) in a wedding. I once heard a sermon at a youth conference on Mordecai's well-known encouragement to Esther that her life may have prepared her "for such a time as this" (Esther 4:14 NRSV). Whenever I mention

Ecclesiastes in public, someone over forty will inevitably start singing The Byrds' classic tune "Turn! Turn! Turn!"

But in terms of real, deep engagement that informs the way we think and live as Christians, these books hardly ever enter into the life of the church or inform the ways that we live our lives in the world. Four of the books (Ecclesiastes, Esther, Lamentations, and Song of Songs) each appear only once in the three-year Revised Common Lectionary cycle that many churches use for their weekly scripture readings.[3] The remaining book, Ruth, appears twice. Even more rarely are these texts actually preached in worship. I can count the number of sermons I've heard on Lamentations without lifting a finger.

These Five Scrolls, which have so enriched the tradition of our Jewish brothers and sisters, have languished in the Christian church. They are gathering dust at the margins of the biblical canon. They have been forgotten.

My purpose in writing this book is to create a space in which these forgotten biblical texts can speak and to see in what ways we might be transformed by the wisdom they have to teach us. I hope to bring these books back from the brink of our forgetfulness to see what word they may have for our contemporary world, both within the church and without it.

As you read, you will see that I try to pay careful attention to the details of each biblical text before offering my thoughts on its significance for today. I think of this practice as trying to be a good listener. It's the same way I try to listen to my friends at Mercy Community Church—or to anyone, really. I try to listen to their stories as carefully as possible. I try to ask good questions. I try to reflect back what I think I'm hearing. Only then, after I have spent some time listening, do I offer my own thoughts and opinions. I try to treat the biblical texts with that same respect, inviting them to speak before offering my own ideas about what they might mean.

Of course, as in any conversation, I can only listen as me. I can only ask the questions that occur to me and can only interpret responses through the listening frameworks that I have. As a result, you will no doubt see that I listen and interpret as a straight, white, middle-class, well-educated, ordained, pastoral, professorial male. I hope you will also see that I have done my best to listen to people who experience the world differently than I do and who therefore read and interpret differently than I do. If you look at the bibliography, you'll see some of the people who have informed my thinking in this book—though of course there are always many more. Along with Jewish scholars, I have tried to pay particular attention to women, people of color, and members of the LGBTQI community in my reading. I hope you will see my indebtedness to them here—and that you will go and read their work, too.

For each biblical text, I have chosen an issue from the contemporary world as a way of framing the conversation. For Song of Songs, I explore human sexuality and the ways the text can invite us to a richer appreciation of sexual desire while also teaching us something about God's desire for us.

I approach Ruth in the context of immigration policy and the status of immigrant communities in the United States. I read Lamentations with questions about the role of anger and protest in the Christian community, particularly regarding police violence and the Black Lives Matter movement. With Ecclesiastes, I explore death anxiety and what it means to live a meaningful life while knowing that we will all inevitably die. Finally, I approach the book of Esther from the issue of white nationalism and the resurgence of ethnic hatred in politics around the globe.

I hope reading this book may open up a little-known part of the Bible to you in new and unexpected ways. These forgotten books have a lot to say. I don't expect you will agree with everything they (or I) have to say, but I do hope they may provoke you to think and act in more theologically rich ways—as they have done for me.

Notes

1. Donny and Fred have given me permission to use their story. I am endlessly grateful to them for this, as for so many things.
2. Translations throughout the book are from the Common English Bible (CEB) unless otherwise noted.
3. See The Revised Common Lectionary, Vanderbilt Divinity Library, http://tinyurl.com/y7uqxx7y. Lamentations also appears once as an optional weekly reading and once in the lectionary for Holy Saturday. Ecclesiastes appears one additional time as the lectionary for New Year's Day.

1

The Song of Songs

Our culture has a sex problem, and the church is partly to blame. From the street to the casting couch to the Oval Office, men feel entitled to women's bodies. Sexualized images of women pervade media and advertising, communicating expectations that women should be sexually available to men. Young girls feel pressure to be "sexy," internalizing unrealistic and unhealthy ideals of the female form. Yet when they perform sexiness too successfully, they may be slut-shamed by their peers. These toxic attitudes about sex and sexuality put lives at risk. The Center for Disease Control (CDC) estimates that nearly half of women and one in four men will experience some form of sexual violence during their lifetime.[1]

In this environment, the church needs to talk about sex, sexuality, and bodies in positive, thoughtful, theologically rich ways. Yet, rather than promoting healthy attitudes toward sex and sexuality, the church too often focuses on restriction and repression, producing guilt and shame rather than helping people embrace the sexual side of being human. Sex and family therapist Tina Schermer Sellers uses the term "religious sexual shame" to describe the complex of dysfunctions arising from Christian purity movements, which teach that all sexual expression outside of marriage is inherently sinful.[2] People raised in such environments, Sellers says, show increased feelings of shame and self-loathing, including depression and risk of death by suicide.

Between the sexual objectification that pervades mainstream culture and the shame-based sexual purity that characterizes much of church culture, there are healthy ways of viewing sex as a mutual, pleasurable, shame-free expression of the joy of being human—as a gift of God, even. Yet, Christians aren't accustomed to thinking of sex and bodies as holy. It's easier to talk about when we should and shouldn't have sex and who we should and shouldn't have sex with. We lack the language to speak of sex as a divine gift or as something that brings us closer to understanding God.

Yet in the Song of Songs, we have a holy book about two young lovers entranced by the allure of human bodies and enthralled by the passion of sexual desire. That the book is even in the Bible has been viewed as scandalous by some. The third-century Christian theologian Origen warned in his *Commentary on the Song of Songs* that all but the most spiritually advanced people should abstain from reading the Song, so powerful is its sexual allure. Yet the great Jewish rabbi Akiva once said,

The whole world is not worth the day on which the Song of Songs was given to Israel; for all the Writings are holy, but the Song of Songs is the holiest of the holy.[3]

Akiva was probably thinking of the traditional interpretation of the Song of Songs as a love story between God and Israel or, for Christians, between Christ and the church. But I like to think Akiva was right about the Song of Songs even in its most literal interpretation. I like to think of the Song of Songs as the holiest of the holy precisely because it invites us to celebrate the goodness of human sexuality, the uninhibited joy of sexual passion, and the intrinsic beauty of the human body in all its shapes, sizes, and skin tones. While the Song of Songs is not perfect, as we will see, I believe it can help us learn to talk about sex, bodies, and God—all in the same holy breath.

Reading the Song of Songs: Setting the Stage

Traditionally, the Song of Songs has been attributed to the great King Solomon, who ruled over Israel in the tenth century BCE. An old rabbinic tradition says that Solomon wrote Song of Songs when he was young, Proverbs in middle age, and Ecclesiastes when he was old.[4] The idea of Solomon as author stems from the superscription of Song of Songs in 1:1, which the King James Version (KJV) translates as "The song of songs, which is Solomon's." However, the Hebrew *le-Shlomo* can mean not only "which is Solomon's" but also "which is for Solomon," as the Common English Bible (CEB) translates. While it is possible that Solomon wrote all or part of the book, most scholars today view the book as a collection of poems written by other authors, whether in Solomon's time or later, that came to be associated with the great king because of his reputation as a writer and lover of women. That is, the book was likely written in the spirit of Solomon rather than by the king himself.

While the book is sometimes called the Song of Solomon, the text calls itself "the Song of Songs" (1:1). The expression in Hebrew is *shir ha-shirim*, which expresses a superlative. In the same way that the Holy of Holies (*qodesh ha-qodeshim*) is the holiest place, the Song of Songs is the songiest of songs. It is the greatest song, or the most sublime song.

One thing that often surprises people about the Song of Songs is that God is not actually mentioned anywhere in the book. Because many Jewish and Christian interpreters have understood the Song to be about the love of God for Israel (or Jesus for the church), you might assume that God is front and center throughout the book. But in fact, Song of Songs is one of only two biblical books that never mention God at all—the other one being Esther.

A Tale of Two Lovers

Far from being a book about God, the Song of Songs celebrates the passion of two young lovers as they seduce each other and enjoy exploring one another's bodies. It celebrates the physical pleasures of sex openly and unashamedly as the two lovers revel in the experience of sexual desire and fulfillment. There is no hint of embarrassment or shame in this text—about bodies or sex or desire. It is simply an affirmation of the joy and excitement of human sexuality.

Because the two lovers are more interested in exploring one another's bodies than filling out their résumés, we know very little about their backgrounds. Though we will come to know them intimately through the course of the book, we don't even know their names. The male lover once refers to the female as "the Shulammite" (6:13), though that isn't, properly speaking, her name. It means "from Jerusalem"—in the way that we might call someone a "New Yorker" or "Bostonian." She typically refers to him as "my love" or "my lover" (6:2–3). Lacking their names, I will use these appellations for the two throughout this chapter: the Shulammite and her lover.

The Shulammite is a dark-skinned, beautiful young woman. She describes herself by saying,

> Dark am I, and lovely, daughters of Jerusalem—
> like the black tents of the Kedar nomads,
> like the curtains of Solomon's palace. (1:5)

Since the Hebrew expression *shechorah 'ani ve-na'vah* can mean either "I am dark *and* lovely" or "I am dark *but* lovely," many English translations have depicted the Shulammite as being embarrassed of her blackness. For instance, the King James Version has her say, "I am black, but comely" (1:5 KJV). Yet, the Shulammite clearly knows she is beautiful, and there is nothing apologetic in her tone. Rather than shame about her skin tone, her claim is that blackness is beautiful—she is a proud, dark-skinned young woman.

We can also surmise that the Shulammite is a girl around the age of puberty, just discovering her sexuality. In a humorous exchange, the Shulammite's brothers describe her as a little girl:

> Our sister is small; she has no breasts.
> What will we do for our sister
> on the day that she is spoken for? (8:8)

They make plans for how they will protect her from boys when she reaches the age of sexual maturity:

> If she is a city wall,
> Then we will build a turret of silver on her.
> And if she is a door,
> then we will barricade her with a panel of cedar. (8:9)

If only they knew what she and her lover are up to!

The Shulammite doesn't see herself as a girl. She declares,

> I'm a city wall,
> and my breasts are the towers. (8:10)

While her brothers think she has no breasts, the Shulammite sees herself as voluptuous, her breasts towering above her body. The contrast suggests that the Shulammite has reached the age where she is just blossoming into womanhood. While her family still thinks of her as their little girl, she has already embraced sexual maturity.

Both the Shulammite and her lover seem to be laborers who work outdoors. The Shulammite keeps her brothers' vineyards (1:6) and tends the goats (1:8). The male lover also seems to be a shepherd (1:7). Their jobs suggest that they come from poor backgrounds and are not royalty, as is sometimes suggested. While she does refer to him twice as a "king" (1:4, 12), this seems to be a playful pet name rather than a biographical detail.

Other than his job, we don't know much about the male lover. We know he has a penchant for bounding over hills (2:8–9; 8:14) and peering out from behind lattices (2:9), suggesting that he is young (and maybe a bit socially awkward), but beyond that we cannot go.

While it is sometimes suggested that the two young lovers are married, there is little in the book to support such a view. The Shulammite still lives at home with her mother and works for her brothers, tending their vineyards. Yet, she knows that she can't bring her lover home to her house. She says,

> If only you were as my brother—
> the one who nursed at my mother's breast.
> I would find you in the street and kiss you,
> and no one would shame me for it.
> I would lead you, I would bring you to my mother's house;
> she would teach me what to do. (8:1–2)

That she longs to bring him to her mother's house—but doesn't—indicates that the family would not approve of their relationship. Further, while the Shulammite desires to kiss her lover in public, she says that she would be shamed for it. Neither her family nor the public can know about their love, suggesting it is secret, unmarried love. The male lover's tendency to stand

> outside our wall,
> peering through the windows,
> peeking through the lattices (2:9)

confirms the point. Far from belonging in the house, he is something of a lurker, hoping to catch his lover's eye as she passes the window but never daring to enter through the front door.

While it is true that the male lover refers to the Shulammite as "my bride" a number of times (4:8, 9, 10, 11, 12; 5:1), this again seems to be a kind of pet name, along with "my dearest" (1:9, 15; 2:10, 13; 4:1, 7; 5:2; 6:4), "my fairest" (2:10, 13), "my dove" (2:14; 5:2; 6:9), and "my perfect one" (5:2; 6:9). In any case, since the full expression is "my sister, my bride" in every case but one (4:8), it seems unwise to take the expression too literally.

The Joy of Sex

To refer to the Song of Songs as a book of erotic poetry may at first sound like a bit of an overstatement. Until one really starts to pay attention, the tale of these young lovers may seem sweet and innocent, like a middle-school crush. This is in part because translators have tended to obscure some of the erotic dimensions of the text in order to make it more "Bible appropriate."

For instance, in the Shulammite's first line in the book, she expresses a desire for her lover that is often translated as

> Let him kiss me with the kisses of his mouth!
> For your love is better than wine. (1:2 NRSV)

This translation suggests that the Shulammite is speaking of the "love" of her male companion as an emotional quality, as though his attitude of tenderness toward her is better than wine. However, the Hebrew word translated as "your love" (*dodekhah*) actually refers not to an emotional quality of love but to a physical one; it would be better translated as "love-making":

> Let him kiss me with the kisses of his mouth!
> For your lovemaking is better than wine (1:2 my translation)

This translation gives a better sense not only of this particular line but also of the framework of the book as a whole. The Song of Songs is fundamentally about the giddiness of young lovemaking.

Yet if we miss the eroticism of Song of Songs, it may not be entirely the fault of translators. The Song itself is subtle in its eroticism, employing sexual innuendo and double entendre to achieve an evasive sexual subtlety. Highly erotic, it is never sexually explicit. The Song of Songs might make you blush, but it won't get you arrested.

In 1:12–14, the Shulammite gives her first description of a sexual liaison with her lover. Her words demonstrate both the subtle eroticism of the poetry and the sheer pleasure of the lovers' encounter. The Shulammite describes it this way:

> While the king was on his couch
> my nard gave off its scent.
> A sachet of myrrh is my lover to me,
> all night between my breasts.
> A cluster of henna, my lover to me,
> in the vineyards of Ein Gedi. (1:12–14 Alter)

In rich, multisensory verse, the Shulammite describes the smell of her perfume enticing her lover on his couch. In the next line, she describes another perfume, myrrh, which she wears in a small satchel around her neck. Then, unexpectedly, the myrrh becomes her lover himself, who now, like the satchel, spends "all night between my breasts." In the following line, the lover then becomes a cluster of henna, now spending the night in the "vineyard of Ein Gedi." The sexual innuendo of him as henna in the vineyard seems clear enough. Yet the poetry remains suggestive, never explicit.

While this description suggests the lovers are in a bed chamber, complete with a couch, it turns out that this entire sexual encounter takes place outside, on a bed of grass spread under the trees. As she concludes her description of this sexual encounter, the Shulammite exclaims,

> Yes, our bed is lush and green!
> The ceilings of our chambers are cedars;
> our rafters cypresses! (1:16b–17)

Our two lovers are nature enthusiasts. We often find them making love in the great outdoors.

A poem in the following chapter describes a sexual liaison that takes place in an orchard (2:3–6). Once again, the description of the orchard merges with the description of the lover. Just as she described him as a sachet of myrrh, she now likens him to an apricot tree in the wood:

> My beloved among the young men
> is a branching apricot tree in the wood.

In that shade I have often lingered, tasting the fruit. (2:3 Bloch and Bloch)

She describes him as the apricot tree, saying she has tasted his fruit. Again, the image is suggestive but not explicit. She continues by describing their lovemaking among the fruit trees:

Let me lie among vine blossoms,
in a bed of apricots!
I am in the fever of love.
His left hand beneath my head,
his right arm holding me close. (2:5–6 Bloch and Bloch)

As the two embrace in a bed of apricot blossoms, his left hand under her head and his right arm embracing her, she finds herself "in the fever of love." I mean, who wouldn't enjoy a little spooning after an afternoon of sex al fresco?

While these two seem to have a serious passion for one another, they also enjoy flirting, often engaging in witty sexual repartee. For instance, in 7:7–8, the male lover says to his companion:

Your stately form resembles a date palm,
and your breasts are like clustered fruit.
I say, "I will climb the palm tree;
I will hold its fruit!"

You can almost see the gleam in his eye when he describes his desire to "climb the tree and hold its fruit."

For her part, the Shulammite returns his flirtatious banter. As he continues

Your palate is like excellent wine . . . (7:9a)

the Shulammite interrupts to finish his thought

> ... flowing smoothly for my love,
> gliding through the lips and teeth. (7:9)

With this give and take, the Shulammite and her lover show that they enjoy not only the passionate side of sex but also the more playful side. They enjoy one another's company, both physically and conversationally, teasing each other and even finishing each other's thoughts.

Mutuality and Consent

In fact, even as the Song celebrates sexual enjoyment, it maintains a remarkably healthy view of consent and mutuality, particularly for such an ancient text.[5] The two lovers invite one another into sexual encounters, and their lovemaking is both consensual and reciprocal. They enjoy each other immensely.

Following the flirtatious encounter I just described, the Shulammite invites her lover to the field, where they will consummate their flirtation:

> Come, my love:
> Let's go out to the field
> and rest all night among the flowering henna.
> Let's set out early for the vineyard.
> We will see if the vines have budded
> and the blossoms opened,
> see if the pomegranates have bloomed.
> There I'll give my loving to you. (7:11–13)

Only after the Shulammite offers herself to her lover, saying

"Let's go out to the field . . . [and] I'll give my loving to you"
does the male lover act on his desire.

This same respectful pattern of invitation and consent
characterizes the two lovers throughout the book. For
instance, in 4:8–16 the male lover expresses his desire for the
Shulammite, describing how she has enticed him. He says,

> You have captured my heart, my sister, my bride!
> You have captured my heart with one glance from your eyes,
> with one strand of your necklace. (4:9)

At the conclusion of his speech, the Shulammite responds to
him saying,

> Let my love come to his garden;
> let him eat its luscious fruit! (4:16)

Only then does he describe their sexual encounter:

> I have come to my garden, my sister, my bride!
> I have gathered my myrrh and my spices.
> I have eaten my honeycomb with honey;
> I have drunk my wine and milk. (5:1)

This is a remarkable illustration of sexual consent, from which
many modern men could learn a great deal.

The two lovers likewise express the mutuality of their relationship in the way they speak of one another. In the opening chapter, as the Shulammite describes her lover as a "sachet
of myrrh . . . lying all night between my breasts," the lover
unexpectedly interjects:

> Look at you—so beautiful, my dearest!
> Look at you—so beautiful! Your eyes are doves! (1:15)

To which the Shulammite immediately responds:

> Look at you—so beautiful, my love!
> Yes, delightful! (1:16)

This spontaneous exchange of mutual admiration is characteristic of the lovers in the Song of Songs. They reciprocate affection, celebrating each other even as they enjoy themselves. Theirs is not selfish or exploitative sexual gratification but mutual desire that fulfills them both. While, as we will see, things are not always so simple in the Song of Songs, this is a good description of the Song as a whole. It celebrates relationships of mutual sexual fulfillment in which both parties are valued and affirmed, desired and fulfilled.

These two young lovers, with their flirtatious, passionate, mutually respectful lovemaking, provide a refreshing counterpoint to the Bible's often negative views of sex and sexuality. Too often the Bible is presented as though it were a stodgy old school marm, wagging a judgmental finger whenever someone thinks sex might be beautiful or pleasurable or—God forbid—fun. Leviticus provides exhaustive lists of who you can and cannot have sex with (your wife, yes! Your mother-in-law, no!). Paul recommends avoiding sex altogether (1 Corinthians 7). But here at last is a biblical text that relishes in human sexuality, joyfully and playfully and without shame. It simply celebrates the pleasure of desire and consummation, of bodies entwined in passionate embrace, of lovemaking pure and simple.

Imagine if this text were to be taken seriously in discussions about biblical views of sex and sexuality. No longer would the conversation be dominated by the sex police who guard the boundaries of "proper" sexual expression, wielding Leviticus and Paul like billy clubs. Song of Songs could make room for those who enjoy sex, who find it pleasurable and beautiful, and who refuse to feel shamed for that enjoyment. It could allow us to speak of desire and pleasure as goods in themselves, affirmed by this holiest of biblical books. If there is a place in the Bible for this unabashed appreciation of sexual enjoyment, surely there could be room in the church as well.

Admiration of the Human Body

Beyond its celebration of human sexuality, a second important aspect of the Song of Songs is its appreciation of the human body, both male and female. At several points, the lovers of the Song simply pause to admire one another's bodies, using a poetic form reminiscent of an Arabic poetic style known as a *watsf*. This poetic form typically describes the body beginning at the head and moving toward the feet, pausing to describe each feature in succession.

There are four such bodily poems in the Song of Songs, three of them describing the female form (4:1–7, 6:4–7, and 7:1–7) and one describing the male (5:10–16). For instance, in 4:1–7 the male describes the Shulammite's body, beginning with her eyes and moving to her hair, teeth, lips, jaw, neck, and breasts.

> Look at you—so beautiful, my dearest!
> Look at you—so beautiful!
> Your eyes are doves

behind the veil of your hair!
Your hair is like a flock of goats
as they stream down Mount Gilead.
Your teeth are like newly shorn ewes
as they come up from the washing pool—
all of them perfectly matched,
not one of them lacks its twin.
Like a crimson ribbon are your lips;
when you smile it is lovely.
Like a slice of pomegranate is the curve of your face
behind the veil of your hair.
Like David's tower is your neck,
splendidly built!
A thousand shields are hung upon it—
all the weapons of the warriors.
Your two breasts are like two fawns,
twins of a gazelle doe,
that graze among the lilies.
. . . .
You are utterly beautiful, my dearest;
there's not a single flaw in you. (4:1–7)

While the significance of some of the imagery is lost on us (what exactly does it mean to have hair like a flock of goats streaming down a mountain or teeth like newly shorn ewes?), the tenderness and affection of the lover's gaze are obvious. He begins and ends his description by declaring her beauty—"So beautiful! So beautiful! You are utterly beautiful!" Importantly, the lover also talks *to* the Shulammite and not *about* her. This isn't locker room talk that sexualizes her body to impress his buddies. Rather, he addresses her directly, as a subject, expressing his admiration and appreciation for her physical form.

In the following chapter, the Shulammite reciprocates by

describing his body, moving from his golden head to his marble thighs:

> His head is finest gold;
> his wavy hair, black as a raven.
> His eyes are like doves
> by channels of water.
> They are bathing in milk,
> sitting by brimming pools.
> His cheeks are like fragrant plantings,
> towers of spices.
> His lips are lilies
> dripping liquid myrrh.
> His arms are gold cylinders
> studded with jewels.
> His belly is smooth ivory
> encrusted with sapphires.
> His thighs are pillars of whitest stone
> set on pedestals of gold.
> His mouth is everything sweet,
> every bit of him is desirable.
> This is my love, this is my dearest,
> daughters of Jerusalem! (5:11–16)

This poem comes at a moment in the Song of Songs when the lover is absent, having disappeared for a moment into the night. She addresses her description to the "daughters of Jerusalem," who have asked her "How is your lover different from any other lover?" (5:9). Conjuring his image before them, the Shulammite describes the contours of his body from memory, carefully recalling the details of his form in loving admiration.

In contrast to a Christian tradition that has too often taught us that bodies are shameful, the Song of Songs revels in the beauty of the human form, both male and female. Yet, in contrast to a culture that exploits (particularly female) bodies as sexualized objects of (particularly male) gratification, the Song remains relational and reciprocal in its admirations of the body. The Song reminds us that human bodies are beautiful, admirable, and worthy of appreciation even as it insists that bodies belong to real people who likewise deserve respect and admiration.

At the same time, as we read these admirations of the body in the Song of Songs, we are no doubt struck by the strangeness of the standards of beauty they reveal. If you don't believe me, try using some of these lines on your next date:

> Your teeth are like newly shorn ewes
> as they come up from the washing pool—
> all of them perfectly matched,
> not one of them lacks its twin. (4:2)
> Your breasts are like two fawns,
> twins of a gazelle doe,
> that graze among the lilies. (4:5)
> [Your] eyes are like doves
> by channels of water.
> They are bathing in milk. (5:12)

Or my particular favorite:

> Your nose is like the tower of Lebanon. (7:4 NRSV)

While these were no doubt the sincerest of admiring compliments in their own time and place, the standards of beauty they reveal clearly no longer pertain in our own culture. What this reveals, of course, is that beauty standards are always cultural constructs—in our own time as much as in biblical times. The standards by which we rate beauty now will seem as arbitrary in the future as the ancient standards of Song of Songs seem to us now. We need not compare ourselves to them.

Rather than aspiring to impossible standards of attractiveness prescribed to us by corporate America, perhaps we can find beauty in bodies of all shapes, sizes, and gender expressions. Maybe we can learn to say to one another—and to ourselves—"You are utterly beautiful my dearest. / There's not a single flaw in you" (4:7).

Women and the Song of Songs

The Song of Songs has been a particularly important book for feminist readers seeking strong female characters in a Bible that often subsumes women into a patriarchal narrative. The Shulammite seems to provide just such a strong female lead. Her voice predominates in the Song of Songs, as she speaks more lines than her male companion. Even more, the Shulammite expresses her sexual desires and passions without any embarrassment or shame. She owns her sexuality. She is the biblical Queen Bey.

Indeed, the Shulammite is a woman-oriented woman. She sees the world as a network of female relationships, in contrast to the patriarchal power structures common in other biblical narratives. She refers to her brothers as "my mother's sons" (1:6 my translation), reversing the usual biblical pattern of identifying relationships through the father. She also refers to her home as "my mother's house" (3:4; 8:2), rather than the usual "father's house," and describes King Solomon as having been crowned by his mother on his wedding day (3:11). Her world is oriented by women.

Yet, other feminist readers sound a word of caution. In her essay "Ten Things Every Feminist Should Know about the Song of Songs," Cheryl Exum warns against an overly romanticized view of the status of women in the Song of Songs. While she recognizes that the Song is positive for women in many ways, she reminds us that it nonetheless reflects an ancient worldview in which men generally had more autonomy than women. While the male lover does often treat the Shulammite as is his equal, he also has a tendency to wander away for periods of time. "Why is this man such an elusive lover?" Exum asks. "He's always off bounding over the hills somewhere, while her fondest wish is to get him inside, to seize him and bring him to her mother's house."[6]

One incident in the Song of Song has been particularly troubling for feminist readers. At the beginning of the scene in 5:2–9, the Shulammite seems to be asleep when she hears her lover knocking. He calls out to her:

> Open to me, my sister, my companion,
> my dove, my innocent!
> For my head is covered with the evening mist,
> my locks with the dew of the night. (5:2 my translation)

The Shulammite playfully responds to her lover through the door,

> I have stripped off my clothes.
> How can I dress again?
> I have bathed my feet.
> How can I dirty them? (5:3 my translation)

She is flirting with him, but her reply has the opposite effect.
Instead her lover pulls away:

> My lover pulls his hand from the latch-hole.
> My body moans for him!
> I arise to open for my lover.
> My hands drip myrrh,
> my fingers liquid myrrh
> upon the handles of the bolt.
> I open for my lover,
> But my lover has withdrawn, passed on.
> How my breath escaped me when he spoke.
> I seek him, but I cannot find him.
> I call to him, but he does not answer. (5:4–6 my translation)

By the time she makes her way to the door, the lover has disappeared into the night. Neither we nor she knows why the lover has vanished—only that he is no longer there when she opens the door.

In the verses that follow, the Shulammite wanders out into the street looking for her departed lover. As she roams the streets alone, she encounters the night watchmen, whose job it should be to protect her. Instead, she says,

> They found me—the guards
> who make their rounds in the city.
> They struck me, bruised me.
> They took my shawl away from me,
> those guards of the city walls! (5:7)

It is unclear precisely why the guards strike and bruise the Shulammite. That they take her shawl suggests that they have exposed her body to shame her if not to sexually assault her. Some have suggested that the guards assume she is a prostitute roaming the streets, beating her without understanding that she is a distraught citizen in need.

The presence of this passage mutes the overall positivity of the Song of Songs for women's self-expression, sexual and otherwise, which we otherwise see celebrated in the book. Even as we recognize the positive, egalitarian messages of the Song of Songs, we need to remain clear-eyed about the places in which it doesn't support women or where it even endangers them. The text is a stark reminder of the perils of being a woman, in both the biblical world and in our own, when venturing out into the streets means risking harm from men—even those sworn to protect.

Laura-Beth Durham, one of my student-colleagues at Hendrix College, took a particular interest in this passage, writing about it in her final paper for my "Race, Gender, Empire, and the Bible" course. While the Bible is not a religious text for Durham, she was intrigued by the parallels she saw between the Shulammite's incident in the street and the dangers faced by many young women today, living in a culture in which nearly half of all women have experienced some form of sexual violence. As a young woman in modern America, Durham resonated with the Shulammite's experience as one that she or her friends might also face.

Finding the lover in the Song unreliable and the other male characters in the text dangerous for women, Durham seeks a woman-positive reading of the book in the bond of sisterhood that, for her, supersedes any relationship to a man—and particularly to a man who has left the Shulammite to wander alone in the streets at night. Durham notices the appearance of the daughters of Jerusalem in 5:9, just after the Shulammite has been struck by the night watchmen. They say to the Shulammite,

What is your beloved more than any other,
O fairest of women?
What is your beloved more than any other,
that you should give us this charge? (5:9)[7]

Durham writes of this encounter, "A reader may envision a group of young women coming upon someone much like themselves, battered, bruised, and cold in the street. As they rush to her aid, lifting her up from the cold stones, she begs for her lover. Then like sisters, they ask her, 'What is your lover more than any other?'"[8]

Durham interprets this inquiry from the daughters of Jerusalem as meaning that no man is worth being abandoned and beaten in the street. There is no man, no matter how wonderful, who is worth such treatment. Rather, for Durham, while the male figures have failed the Shulammite, the women of the city remain constant. "For women, we can hold onto the bonds of sisterhood between the Maidens of Jerusalem and the Bride, and support each other in the event of sexual assault," she writes. "We must lift each other up, and be unafraid to point out to each other when the men in our lives are possessive. We must be unafraid to ask 'Who is your beloved more than any other?'"

One might add that the priority of sisterhood ought to guide our reading of the Song of Songs as a whole. Where the Song supports the full thriving of women, as it often does, we can celebrate it and admire its beauty. But where the Song abandons women or leaves them vulnerable, our priority must be protecting and uplifting our sisters.

The Allegorical Reading

So far, I have been looking at the Song of Songs as love poetry expressing sexual desire between two young lovers. Yet over the centuries most interpreters, both Jewish and Christian, have read the Song as an allegory describing the love between God and humanity. The term *allegory* refers to the hidden meaning of a text—what appears to be about one thing is understood as being about something else entirely. In the Jewish allegorical reading of the Song, the male character has been understood as God and the female as Israel. In the Christian allegory, the male is Christ and the female either the church or the individual believer.

As an example of the theological potential for an allegorical reading, we can transpose the passage in 2:3–6, which I earlier read as a love poem, into the divine register, as an expression of the relationship between God and humanity. An allegorical reading transforms the Shulammite's statement that "like an apricot tree among the wild trees, so is my lover among the young men" (2:3a) into a claim about God's value as opposed to other gods, whether real or imagined. Her subsequent statement "I delight in his shade, and I linger there" (2:3b) now bespeaks the rest and protection that is possible in God. Her declaration "He brings me into his banqueting table; his banner over me is love" now describes God as sustaining humanity with the bounteousness of creation and proudly waving a flag over us to claim us as God's own.

One of the most beautiful aspects of the allegorical interpretation is the image in 2:6, "His left arm is beneath my head; his right hand embraces me." Read allegorically, this verse becomes an image of God's intimate love for humanity. With one hand under our head and the other embracing us, God wraps us up in loving, godly arms and holds us, protecting and comforting us as we rest.

Because of God's radical love for each of us, we cannot be separated from God, even by the power of death. The Shulammite's words

> Set me as a seal over your heart,
> as a seal upon your arm,
> for love is as strong as death,
> passionate love unrelenting as the grave (8:6)

become a plea for resurrection. If we are sealed on God's heart, on God's arm, God will not forget us, and God's love will reach even beyond the grave to restore us to life.

Yet, for all its beauty, the allegorical interpretation is not without its problems. The difficulty encountered by the allegorical interpretation is the same identified by feminist critics concerning the status of women in the Song. If humanity (or Israel or the church) is to be identified with the Shulammite, then the same dangers that face women in the literal reading of Song of Songs threaten humanity (or Israel or the church) in the allegorical reading. What does it mean to worship a

God who disappears intermittently, bounding away over the hills? What does it mean to rely on a God who abandons us in the middle of the night if we are too slow to respond? What does it mean to seek a God who leaves us to be beaten by the watchmen roaming the city?

One response to the quandary is to follow the lead of the ancient rabbis, who viewed the Song of Songs as an allegory of the history of Israel since the exodus. The Aramaic Targum of the Song of Songs interprets the Shulammite's assault as a reference to the Babylonian exile.[9] Because Israel wouldn't repent, God removed the divine presence from them and handed them over to Nebuchadnezzar. The guards in the streets represent the Babylonians, who carry Israel away into captivity, where they cry out for God, their Beloved.

On this reading, God's history is not one of constancy. God's history is more like the story of the male lover in the Song of Songs, who loves passionately but intermittently, who becomes angry and disappears into the night.

An Alternative Allegorical Reading

However, there is another way of reading the allegory that may have richer theological implications for today. A pastor friend of mine, Marie Mainard O'Connell, suggests reversing the poles of the allegory, reading the Shulammite as God and the male companion as humanity. Mainard O'Connell is one of the pastors at the church I attend as well as one of the cofounders of Mercy Community Church of Little Rock, a small worshiping community consisting mostly of people who live on the streets. She is also an activist in our community who served as the chaplain of the local Occupy movement and fought the state legislature when it tried to legalize discrimination against the LGBTQI community. As a clergywoman, Mainard O'Connell embodies in female form the love of God for the world. Why couldn't the Shulammite do the same?

Following Mainard O'Connell's suggestion transforms the allegorical reading of the Song of Songs. Now, rather than God being the male lover off gallivanting around the hills, God is the Shulammite, waiting patiently for us to return from our wanderings. We can imagine God saying of us,

> I looked for the one whom I love with all my heart.
> I looked for him but couldn't find him.
> "I will rise now and go all around the city,
> through the streets and the squares.
> I will look for the one whom I love with all my heart." (3:1b–2)

God no longer wanders away as in the traditional allegorical reading. Rather, God is the constant one. God is the one who waits for us, who longs for us when we wander away, who scours the streets of the city seeking us. God loves us "with all my heart."

If we extend this reverse allegory to the story of the midnight beating of the Shulammite, we find that God is no longer the one who hands us over to others to be beaten, as in the first allegorical interpretation. Rather, God is the one who risks being beaten on our behalf, who ventures into the dark night seeking us, risking the Divine Self. For Christian readers, this interpretation has obvious resonances with the story of Jesus, who risked being beaten and crucified in order to seek us out, lost as we were in the darkness of sin and death.

So, too, does reading the Shulammite as God change the significance of other passages in the Song. When we hear God (as the Shulammite) saying,

I belong to my lover,
and [my lover] belongs to me (6:3)

this means something different than when we say it of God. For us to say that we belong to God and God belongs to us is a statement of faith. We entrust ourselves to God and believe God is for us. But when God (as the Shulammite) says these words to us, it means something far more radical. For God to say, "I belong to my lover, and [my lover] belongs to me" is a divine affirmation of God's prior faithfulness. God claims us first. The belonging is God's doing, not ours. We are claimed by God because of God's love for us, not as a matter of faith but as a matter of divine certainty. God has said so.

Similarly when we read the words

Set me as a seal over your heart,
as a seal upon your arm,
for love is as strong as death,
passionate love unrelenting as the grave. (8:6)

as being spoken by God, the significance is likewise transformed. While in the original allegory, these words were humanity asking God to remember us when we die, in the reverse allegory they become God's assurances that God will never forget us, even when we die. God tells us to set God as a

seal on our hearts, on our arms, to remind us of God's endur-
ing love for us. We never need to doubt that God's love is as
strong as death, as unrelenting as the grave. We can believe
it. We can seal it on our hearts. God's love for us knows no
bounds.

Reading the Song of Songs for Today

Which way *should* we read the Song of Songs—as a book
of love poetry, as an allegory of God and humanity, or as a
reverse allegory of humanity and God? The beauty of this
text (and arguably of all biblical texts) is that there is much
to be gained by reading it in all of these ways. We need
not decide among the various interpretive approaches which
one is "the best." Rather, the Bible is always richer than any
one interpretation can grasp. By reading the text in all of
these ways—exploring them, overlapping them, juxtaposing
them—we can learn much about ourselves, about God, and
about our relationship to the Divine.

Reading the Song of Songs as a book of love poetry gives
biblical expression to the goodness of human sexuality, an
emphasis that is too often lost in both the contemporary
church and in the culture at large. It is odd that in a Christian
culture often obsessed with issues of sex and sexuality, the
Song of Songs is rarely brought into the discussion. Perhaps
it is our discomfort with sex that leads us to ignore the Song
of Songs, focusing instead on texts that regulate or control
sexuality. Or perhaps it is that our ignorance of the Song of
Songs contributes to our discomfort with sex, limiting our

theological language for discussing sexuality in thoughtful ways. The Song of Songs reminds us that the "biblical perspective" on sex and sexuality is not merely about anxiety, purity, and restriction but also about desire, enjoyment, and the full expression of our sexual selves.

If we read the Song of Songs allegorically, with God in the role of the male lover, we find a God who loves humanity passionately, who embraces us and says, "You are utterly beautiful, my dearest. / There's not a single flaw in you" (4:7). If we read God as the female lover, we find a God who claims us before we claim her, who seeks us when we wander away from her, who seals it upon our hearts that the love of God is stronger than death.

If we read these layers simultaneously—embracing both the sexuality and the allegory of the text—we find that there is in fact something divine about human sexuality. Not only is it good and pleasurable in its own right, but it is also capable of expressing the love between God and humanity. Far from being shameful or unspeakable in polite company, human sexuality gives expression to the passionate love of God for humanity. Nothing else can express the urgency, passion, and intimacy of God's love for us.

Notes

1. M. J. Breiding, S. G. Smith, K. C. Basile, M. L. Walters, J. Chen, and M. T. Merrick, "Prevalence and Characteristics of Sexual Violence, Stalking, and Intimate Partner Violence Victimization—National Intimate Partner and Sexual Violence Survey, United States, 2011," *Surveillance Summaries* 63, no. 8 (September 5, 2014): 1–18.

2. Tina Schermer Sellers, *Sex, God, and the Conservative Church: Erasing Shame from Sexual Intimacy* (New York: Routledge, 2017), Kindle.

3. *Mishnah Yadaim* 3:5. Translation in Sid Z. Leiman, *The Canonization of Hebrew Scripture: The Talmudic and Midrashic Evidence*, 2nd ed., Transactions of the Connecticut Academy of Arts and Sciences 47 (New Haven: Connecticut Academy of Arts and Sciences, 1991), 106.

4. *Song of Songs Rabbah*, 1.10

5. This discussion is indebted to J. Cheryl Exum, *Song of Songs: A Commentary*, The Old Testament Library (Louisville: Westminster John Knox, 2005), loc. 621, Kindle.

6. J. Cheryl Exum, "Ten Things Every Feminist Should Know about the Song of Songs," in *The Song of Songs: A Feminist Companion to the Bible (Second Series)*, ed. Athalya Brenner and Carole R. Fontaine (Sheffield: Sheffield Academic, 2000), 30; italics in original.

7. Translation is from the New English Bible (NEB).

8. Laura-Beth Durham, "Victim-Blaming in the Song of Solomon" (undergraduate paper, Hendrix College, 2017). Used by permission.

9. For an English translation, see Philip S. Alexander, *The Targum of Canticles*, Aramaic Bible 17A (Collegeville, MN: Liturgical, 2003).

2

Ruth

In her book *Killing the American Dream*, journalist and author Pilar Marrero traces the rise of anti-immigrant sentiment in the United States over the past thirty years. Marrero, who herself immigrated to the United States from Venezuela in the 1980s, laments,

> At this point of the twenty-first century, the United States is a country that idealizes its immigrant origins but cannot understand the importance of its present-day immigrants. For the first time in recent history, the United States of America is becoming a country that is hostile to the newly arrived. Laws and immigration politics are controlled by extremist minorities who manipulate public opinion and who have successfully blocked the passage of measures meant to integrate these newest Americans. The fact that the most recent arrivals are only slightly or in no way different from their own immigrant ancestors is something the extremists conveniently leave out of the conversation.[1]

America's strength has always been its immigrants, Marrero argues, and if we are to have a prosperous future it will be "thanks to, not in spite of, its immigrants."[2] Yet increasing suspicion of immigrants, enshrined in laws such as Arizona's SB 1070, which permits law enforcement to detain any person who presents a "reasonable suspicion" of being undocumented, makes the culture increasingly hostile to immigrants—and even to those who are thought to "look like" foreigners, though they may have been here for generations.

The book of Ruth provides fertile ground for theological reflection on the role of immigrants in American society. Written during a period of rising anti-foreigner nationalism in the land of Judah, it tells the story of a Moabite immigrant whose dedication to her Israelite mother-in-law saves the family line of Israel's greatest king, David. Along the way, the book raises important issues related to the role of immigrants in society, as well as the dangers they face trying to survive in a foreign land.

Reading Ruth: Setting the Stage

The book of Ruth takes place "during the days when the judges ruled" (1:1)—that is, between the time the Israelites escaped from slavery in Egypt and the rise of Israelite monarchy several centuries later. Yet, scholars agree that the book of Ruth itself was written later. One plausible context for the writing of the book is during the period of Persian rule, after the fall of the monarchy and the ensuing exile in Babylonia, as the Judean deportees were returning to reestablish themselves in the region of Judah (ca. fifth century BCE).

According to the books of Ezra and Nehemiah, that period was characterized by a strong anti-immigrant sentiment

among at least some of the population. As the people returning from exile sought to rebuild their nation, they began to
blame their national woes on the presence of immigrants in
the community. The book of Ezra describes some community leaders coming to Ezra to complain that

> the people of Israel, the priests, and the Levites haven't kept
> themselves separate from the peoples of the neighboring lands
> with their detestable practices. . . . They've taken some of their
> daughters as wives for themselves and their sons, and the holy
> descendants have become mixed with the neighboring peoples.
> (Ezra 9:1–2)

Viewing this ethnic mixing as the source of their troubles,
the people declare that they will "make a covenant with our
God to send away all these wives and their children" (Ezra
10:2–3a). The book closes with all of the foreign wives and
their children being deported back to their homelands, leaving the land of Judah ethnically purified.

The central character of the book of Ruth is just such a
woman who would have been targeted for deportation by the
communities reflected in Ezra and Nehemiah had she lived in
their day. She is not just a foreigner but specifically a Moabite,
as the book repeatedly reminds us (Ruth 1:22, 2:2, 2:6, 2:21,
4:5, 4:10), and she is married to an Israelite—precisely the
kind of intermarriage opposed by Ezra and Nehemiah.

The Moabites often came in for sharp criticism in the
rhetoric of ancient Israel. According to Genesis, they were
descendants of Lot, a nephew of the Israelites' ancestor Abraham. Lot and his daughters had escaped the destruction of
Sodom and settled in the hills of Zoar, where they were

living isolated in a cave. Lacking available men, Lot's daughters schemed to get their father drunk and have sex with him. The resulting children were Ammon, the ancestor of the Ammonites, and Moab, the ancestor of the Moabites, including—many generations later—Ruth. The repeated reference to Ruth as a Moabite also conjures a whole host of other biblical traditions about animosity between the Israelites and the Moabites.[3] Chief among these is the Deuteronomic law that "Moabites can't belong to the Lord's assembly" (Deuteronomy 23:3).

Given this background, we may read the book of Ruth as a story composed in the time of Ezra and Nehemiah in order to engage a cultural dispute concerning the status of immigrants and foreigners in postexilic Judah. Read in that context, the book of Ruth provides a counterpoint to the prevailing attitudes reflected in the books of Ezra and Nehemiah. Rather than viewing foreign women as dangerous and intermarriage as destructive to the community, the book of Ruth promotes a positive view of immigrants and foreigners, including even the Moabite women who seem to be so greatly feared in the culture reflected by Ezra and Nehemiah.

The book of Ruth also engages cultural disputes about immigrants and foreigners in our own time. From discriminatory policing laws to the refusal of refugees from war-torn countries, from the travel ban to DACA to the border wall, we find ourselves in a time of national crisis about the status of immigrants and foreigners. As it speaks to the anti-immigrant sentiment of Ezra-Nehemiah, the book of Ruth may speak to our time as well.

The Death of a Family

The book of Ruth opens on a refugee crisis. Facing a famine in their hometown of Bethlehem, the Israelites Naomi and Elimelech flee to Moab with their two sons, Mahlon and Chilion. Taking refuge in a foreign land, they make a life for themselves. The two sons marry Moabite women, Ruth and Orpah, and they settle in Moab. After some years, Elimelech dies, followed shortly by his two sons, leaving Naomi alone with her two Moabite daughters-in-law. Really, Naomi and Elimelech should have known better than to name their sons Mahlon (Heb. *machlon*), which hints at the Hebrew word for "sickness" (*machalah*), and Chilion (Heb. *chilyon*), which resembles the word for "annihilation" (*chillayon*). It's like naming your kids Sicky Sickerson and Deathy McDeathface. Don't do it. They will die.

The deaths of Elimelech and his sons leave Naomi and her daughters-in-law vulnerable in a culture in which women typically depended on men for survival. The vulnerability of widows and foreigners underlies the biblical laws commanding special care for "the immigrants, the orphans, and the widows," who relied on the care of the community to survive (Deuteronomy 24:18–21). Separated from their community, and with no husbands or sons to support them, it's unclear how the women will survive.

Yet for all the uncertainty about survival, Naomi's greatest tragedy may be the extinction of Elimelech's family line. In a culture that didn't believe in a literal afterlife, leaving children to carry on the family name was essential to surviving death. A person could, in a sense, live on in their children and their continued connection to the community of Israel. Dying childless meant being cut off from the community altogether, as though you had never been.

So concerned were the ancient Israelites about the continuation of the family line that they practiced what is known as the *law of levirate marriage* (Deuteronomy 25:5–10). That law states that if a man dies with no children, his brother has an obligation to marry the dead man's wife and produce a son "so that his brother's legacy will not be forgotten in Israel" (Deuteronomy 25:6). But Elimelech and both of his sons have died, leaving no children to carry on their legacy. Thus, Naomi has not only suffered the tragic loss of her husband and sons, but she must also live with the knowledge that they will be cut off from the future of Israel, forgotten by the passage of time. Their family line has been erased, with no apparent way to restore it.

Hearing that God has again blessed the land of Judah with food, Naomi begins the long journey homeward, where she may live out her days as a widow in the care of her community. While she intends to go alone, both Ruth and Orpah set out to follow her. Naomi protests,

> Go, turn back, each of you to the household of your mother. May the Lord deal faithfully with you, just as you have done with the dead and with me. May the Lord provide for you so

that you may find security, each woman in the household of her husband. (1:8–9)

Naomi blesses her daughters-in-law in the name of Israel's God, praying that God will "deal faithfully" (1:8) with them and "provide" (1:9) for them. Yet there is a subtle irony to Naomi's words. When she prays for God to "deal faithfully with you as you have done with the dead and with me," she prays that God might become more like her Moabite daughters-in-law. While Naomi believes God has not been faithful to her, Ruth and Orpah have. She thinks even God could learn a thing or two from these foreign women.

The Faithfulness of a Foreigner

At first, both Ruth and Orpah insist they will stay with Naomi, neither returning to their mother's house (1:10), but Naomi encourages them a second time to return to their people:

> Turn back, my daughters. Why would you go with me? Will there again be sons in my womb, that they would be husbands for you? Turn back, my daughters. Go. I am too old for a husband. If I were to say that I have hope, even if I had a husband tonight, and even more, if I were to bear sons—would you wait until they grew up? Would you refrain from having a husband? No, my daughters. This is more bitter for me than for you, since the Lord's will has come out against me. (1:11–13)

Naomi's words reflect her hopelessness about the future. She believes that "the Lord's will has come out against me" (1:13), so that there is no possibility of restoration. Because Naomi believes that security can only be found in the company of husbands and sons, she sees no way forward for herself. Opportunity for her daughters-in-law, she believes, lies not on her path but in the security of other marriages, other husbands, and other sons.

Orpah now decides to return to her home and to her people, weeping and kissing Naomi as she departs. Yet Ruth determines to stay with Naomi, pledging her undying loyalty to Naomi with some of the best-known words of the Bible:

> Where you go, I will go; and wherever you stay, I will stay. Your people will be my people, and your God will be my God. Wherever you die, I will die, and there I will be buried. May the Lord do this to me and more so if even death separates me from you. (1:16–17)

Ruth's words bespeak such deep commitment that they have long been a model for Christian marriages, used in many traditional wedding services. Yet these words are not about heterosexual marriage but about the commitment of one woman to another. They stand witness to the deep, lifelong, committed love that is possible between two women—and indeed between any two people. Even the word used in 1:14 to describe how Ruth "clung" (*davaqah*) to Naomi is the same word used in Genesis 2:24 to describe marriage as a man clinging (*davaq*) to his wife. While Naomi envisions the future only in terms of men, Ruth affirms the power and possibility of women-oriented women.

Ruth's words also demonstrate the deep loyalty that this young Moabite woman has to her Israelite mother-in-law. Her devotion runs so deep that she will leave her home, give up her people, and worship Naomi's god in order to be with her. For this reason, the story of Ruth is celebrated in Jewish tradition as the story of the first convert to Judaism. Though she is a Moabite, Ruth claims full devotion to the religion and culture of her Israelite mother-in-law.

Homecoming

As Naomi approaches her hometown of Bethlehem with her Moabite daughter-in-law, the two of them cause quite a stir. While the Common English Bible (CEB) says that "the whole town was excited on account of them" (1:19), the verse might better be translated as "the town was buzzing" about them. It must have been quite a sight, Naomi returning home after more than a decade away, without her husband or sons, but with a Moabite woman following alongside. "Can this be Naomi?" the women of the town inquire (1:19). Their question may signify excitement at seeing their long-lost relative or dismay at her pitiful state—likely it indicates both. Notably, no one mentions Ruth.

Naomi responds to the women's query by asking them to call her by a different name:

> Don't call me Naomi, but call me Mara, for the Almighty has made me very bitter. I went away full, but the Lord has returned me empty. Why would you call me Naomi, when the Lord has testified against me, and the Almighty has deemed me guilty? (1:20–21)

Other biblical characters also undergo name changes at pivotal moments in their lives. In Genesis, God changes Abram's name to Abraham and Sarai's name to Sarah as a sign of God's promise to them (Genesis 17:5). God changes Jacob's name to Israel because he "struggled with God and with men and won" (Genesis 32:28). Yet, Naomi's name change differs from these in two important ways. First, the change from Naomi ("pleasantness") to Mara ("bitterness") indicates not a blessing but a curse. Second, whereas God changes the names of the other characters, Naomi is left to change her own name. God is nowhere to be found.

There is also some irony in Naomi's description of herself as returning from Moab "empty" (*reyqam*). While she has indeed lost her husband and sons, her daughter-in-law Ruth stands beside her, unacknowledged by either Naomi or the women of the town. Though Naomi doesn't yet understand the value of Ruth for her survival, Ruth has committed herself to Naomi. As it turns out, the devotion of this Moabite woman will be more than enough to fill Naomi's life again.

Gleaning the Fields

After Naomi and Ruth arrive in Bethlehem, the narrator introduces a new character into the story saying,

> Naomi had a respected relative, a man of worth, through her husband from the family of Elimelech. His name was Boaz. (2:1)

The appearance of a male relative offers a glimmer of hope in the story, though it isn't clear at this point exactly how Boaz will be significant. Some interpreters have mistakenly thought that Boaz, as a male relative, has a duty to provide a male heir for his deceased relative, Elimelech. However, that view misunderstands the law of levirate marriage, which applies only to brothers and doesn't extend to more distant relatives such as Boaz (Deuteronomy 25:5–10).

For now, the future seems to be up to Ruth. A despondent Naomi has disengaged, offering no way forward for the two women. Ruth initiates the story of their survival, announcing to Naomi that she will go to the fields to "glean among the ears of grain behind someone in whose eyes I find favor" (2:2).

Although she is a foreigner, Ruth demonstrates a thorough understanding of Israelite law and customs. She knows that the Torah requires wealthier Israelites to provide food for the widows, orphans, and foreigners in their midst. Leviticus instructs,

> When you harvest your land's produce, you must not harvest all the way to the edge of your field; and don't gather every remaining bit of your harvest. Leave these items for the poor and the immigrant. (Leviticus 23:22; see also Leviticus 19:9–10)

Deuteronomy makes a similar command:

> Whenever you are reaping the harvest of your field and you leave some grain in the field, don't go back and get it. Let it go to the immigrants, the orphans, and the widows so that the Lord your God bless you in all that you do. . . . Remember how you were a slave in Egypt. That's why I'm commanding you to do this thing. (Deuteronomy 24:19–22)

This is the Torah's version of a social safety net. While growers could surely reap higher profits by gathering up all the produce of their fields, God commands that they forego some of their own gain in order to care for the most vulnerable. God reminds the Israelites that they were once exploited in a foreign land and commands them not to do the same to others.

Ruth the Moabite, knowing that the Israelites' founding documents command the protection of widows and immigrants like herself, heads to the fields in search of a benefactor. The narrator tells us that Ruth finds herself in the field of Naomi's relative Boaz "by chance" (2:3). When Boaz arrives at the field, he immediately inquires after Ruth, asking, "To whom does this young woman belong?" (2:5). The overseer responds,

> She's a young Moabite woman, the one who returned with Naomi from the territory of Moab. She said, "Please let me glean so that I might gather grain from among the bundles behind the harvesters." She arrived and has been on her feet from the morning until now, and has sat down for only a moment. (2:6–7)

The overseer twice identifies Ruth as a foreigner—the Moabite woman from Moab. While he mentions that she "returned with Naomi," he doesn't mention that she is Naomi's daughter-in-law or that she is the widow of Boaz's relative Mahlon. Rather, she remains just "a young Moabite woman" (2:6). He commends her work ethic, noting that she has only just sat down for a rest.

According to the overseer, Ruth has requested "to gather grain from among the bundles behind the harvesters" (2:7). There is some debate as to precisely what this means. Most likely, she has asked to follow behind the reapers, gathering the standing stalks they have passed over and gathering them into bundles.[4] If so, she has simply requested to do what is already permitted for widows and foreigners by the Torah law. If that's the case, then Ruth has demonstrated that she not only knows the Israelite law but that she also respects the generosity of the landowners. She doesn't simply take what she is legally permitted to take. She asks permission to do so.

From the beginning Boaz takes an interest in her, inviting her to remain in his field rather than moving on to another. He says,

> Don't go glean in another field; don't go anywhere else. Instead, stay here with my young women. Keep your eyes on the field that they are harvesting and go along after them. I've ordered the young men not to assault you. Whenever you are thirsty, go to the jugs and drink from what the young men have filled. (2:8–9)

Rather than leaving her to fend for herself, he sends her to glean behind his female harvesters, warns the male harvesters not to bother her, and offers her water from jugs that she doesn't have to fill herself.

Boaz has no legal obligation to do any of these things for her, and she takes notice. She inquires why he has shown her special favor, since "I'm an immigrant" (2:10). As it turns out, Boaz has already heard of Ruth and the loyalty that she has shown to his relative Naomi. He acknowledges the sacrifices she has made, "how you left behind your father, your mother, and the land of your birth" to stay with Naomi (2:11). In gratitude, Boaz calls upon God to bless her:

> May the Lord reward you for your deed. May you receive a rich reward from the Lord, the God of Israel, under whose wings you have come to seek refuge. (2:12)

In wishing her safety under God's wings (*kenafim*), Boaz invokes an image familiar from the Psalms. For instance, the psalmist prays that God will "hide me in the protection of your wings" (Psalm 17:8) and declares that "I take refuge in the shadow of your wings until destruction passes by" (Psalm 57:1).

While Ruth presumably appreciates Boaz's prayer for God's protection, she has more practical things in mind. She wants protection—not from God but from Boaz himself. With great subtlety, she replies,

> May I continue to find favor in your eyes, sir, because you've comforted me and because you've spoken kindly to your female servant—even though I'm not one of your female servants. (2:13)

The term Ruth uses for "female servant" (*shifchah*) describes a female servant at the lowest rung of the household—responsible for the most menial tasks, but a member of the household nonetheless.[5] Since she currently has the status of a widowed immigrant, to be a *shifchah* would be an improvement, at least connecting her to a household. As soon as she makes the suggestion, she immediately withdraws it, declaring that she is "not one of your female servants." Astutely, she manages to make a bold request while not appearing to consider herself above her station. She is, after all, just "an immigrant" (2:10).

Boaz doesn't respond immediately to her words. Yet at the

midday meal, he does invite her to sit with the harvesters, serving her bread and roasted grain until she has her fill. He then instructs his young men,

> Let her glean between the bundles, and don't humiliate her. Also, pull out some from the bales for her and leave them behind for her to glean. And don't scold her. (2:14–16)

Boaz has now given her permission to glean not only "*among* the bundles" (*ba-'omarim*), as before, but also "*between* the bundles" (*beyn-'omarim*), seemingly a special privilege reserved for members of the family.[6] By granting Ruth the privileges of sitting with the harvesters and gleaning between the bundles, Boaz accepts her request to be treated as a servant of his household.

Through her knowledge of the law, her respect of local customs, and her quick-witted use of language, Ruth the Moabite has managed to find some measure of security for herself and for her mother-in-law, Naomi. While their problems aren't yet resolved, they at least have food on the table.

A Hope for Redemption

Ruth returns home at the end of the day with about five gallons of grain and her leftovers from the midday meal. Impressed, Naomi asks whose field Ruth has been working in for the day. When she learns it was Boaz, Naomi declares a blessing for him:

> May he be blessed by the Lord, who hasn't abandoned his faithfulness with the living or the dead. (2:20)

Naomi tells Ruth that Boaz "is one of our close relatives; he's one of our redeemers" (2:20). Repeating and expanding on the narrator's earlier introduction of Boaz (2:1), Naomi now refers to him not just as a relative but also as a redeemer.

The term *redeemer* (Heb. *go'el*) has a specific legal meaning in the Hebrew Bible. According to Leviticus:

> When one of your fellow Israelites faces financial difficulty and must sell part of their family property, his redeemer [*go'el*] will come and buy back [*ga'al*] what their fellow Israelite has sold. (Leviticus 25:25 CEB adapted)

The redeemer has the responsibility to purchase the property of a close relative who has fallen into poverty. By doing so, the redeemer allows the impoverished person to become financially stable while the land still remains in the family. The redeemer would return the land either when the impoverished family member could afford to buy it back or at the Year of Jubilee, when all property was to be returned to its original owner (Leviticus 25:8–10). Though we don't learn of it until later in the text (Ruth 4:3), it turns out that Naomi has a piece of land belonging to Elimelech that she can redeem in order to provide long-term security for herself. She just needs a family member who can redeem it.

With this information, we can now see two possible roles for Boaz in the outcome of the story. He may function as a redeemer for Naomi, purchasing her land and bringing it into his household. As a relative of Elimelech, he might also take Ruth as a wife, perhaps even providing an heir for Elimelech—though, as we have seen, he has no legal obligation to do so. The question for the rest of the text is how all of this will play out.

A Proposal at the Threshing Floor

At the end of the harvest season, Naomi conceives of a plan to get Ruth and Boaz together. At last beginning to take some initiative in the events unfolding around her, Naomi declares to Ruth that she will "seek security for you, so that things might go well for you" (3:1). Naomi doesn't mention herself, claiming only to seek protection for Ruth. While it is possible to read her plan as devious (manipulating Ruth to get to Boaz), I prefer to read Naomi as genuinely seeking Ruth's security with no particular thought of herself, as when she tried to send Ruth home in 1:11–13.

Naomi instructs her daughter-in-law,

> Tonight he will be winnowing barley at the threshing floor. You should bathe, put on some perfume, wear some nice clothes, and go down to the threshing floor. Don't make yourself known to the man until he has finished eating and drinking. When he lies down, notice the place where he is lying. Then go, uncover his feet, and lie down. And he will tell you what to do. (3:2–4)

The plan is strikingly forward. The threshing floor was the place where men labored to separate the harvested grain from the chaff. According to the prophet Hosea, it was also a place of prostitution (Hosea 9:1). A well-dressed, perfumed woman at the threshing floor smacks of scandal.

Naomi instructs Ruth to wait until after dark, when Boaz has eaten and drunk, and then to go to where he is sleeping.

The phrase translated "uncover his feet" can be interpreted several different ways. Some scholars, noting that "feet" (*reglayim*) can serve as a euphemism for male genitalia in the Hebrew Bible, suggest that Ruth is to uncover Boaz's genitals. Others, noting that Naomi doesn't use the word *reglayim* but the related word, *margelot*, which refers to the place where Boaz's feet are resting, suggest that Ruth is to uncover *herself* and lie at Boaz's feet.[7] Whatever the case, it is clear that Naomi has instructed Ruth to wait for Boaz to go to sleep and then to uncover either him or herself, waiting for him to tell her what to do. Either way, the sexual implications are clear.

Ruth carries out the plan exactly as instructed. Well—almost. As we will see, rather than waiting for Boaz to tell her what to do, Ruth makes two requests of her own, asking Boaz both to marry her and to act as Naomi's redeemer (*go'el*).

Following Naomi's instructions, Ruth makes her way to the threshing floor and watches as Boaz eats and drinks until he is "in a good mood" (3:7). He has a nice, happy buzz at the end of a long day of work. After he lies down to sleep at the edge of the grain pile, Ruth makes her way over to him and uncovers whatever she uncovers. In the middle of the night, Boaz awakes with a start, realizing there is a woman lying next to him. "Who are you?" he asks (3:9).

The scene is probably meant to be comical. Boaz has awakened from a drunken sleep only to find a Moabite woman lying next to him with various pieces of clothing removed.

Recalling the origin story of the Moabites, in which one of Lot's daughters gets him drunk and has sex with him while he is asleep (Genesis 19:30–38), we imagine Boaz being uncertain about what may have happened during the night. He was drunk. At least one of them is naked. How many explanations can there be? While we know Boaz hasn't slept with Ruth, Boaz can't be so sure.

Yet, when Boaz asks Ruth who she is, Ruth deviates from Naomi's advice and takes things into her own hands. Rather than waiting for Boaz to tell her what to do, she tells *him* what to do. She says,

> I'm Ruth your servant. Spread out your robe over your servant.

And then she adds,

> Surely[8] you are a redeemer. (3:9)

For all its brevity, Ruth's statement is pregnant with significance. First, she refers to herself using not the term for a lower-class servant (*shifchah*) as before but the term *'amah*, which refers to a higher-class servant who is eligible for marriage.[9] Further, when she asks Boaz to "spread out your robe over your servant," she uses the same Hebrew word (*kanaf*) that Boaz had used when blessing her with protection by God's wings (*kenafim*) in 2:12. The phrase "spread out your robe" also indicates a covenantal commitment of marriage, as in Ezekiel 16:8. Thus, Ruth has asked Boaz to take her as his wife, using his own words about God's protection to indicate that, for her, God's protection can't be separated from the protection of marriage to Boaz.

Additionally, in the second half of her statement, Ruth reminds Boaz that he is a redeemer (*go'el*) for Naomi. Many translations, including the CEB, connect the issue of the redeemer to the issue of marriage: "Spread out your robe over your servant, *because* you are a redeemer." However, as we have seen, there is no apparent connection between being a redeemer and marriage. In fact, if Boaz had a legal obligation as redeemer to marry Ruth, the entire threshing-floor seduction would have been unnecessary. They could simply have taken Boaz to court. Rather, Ruth is raising a second, separate issue involving Boaz's responsibility to act as a redeemer in order to purchase Naomi's land in accordance with the redemption law in Leviticus 25:25.[10]

Ruth has thus made two requests at once—one asking Boaz to marry her and the other asking him to redeem Naomi's property. Ruth the Moabite seems to have figured out a complex legal way to marry Boaz while also retaining her connection to Naomi, which she had earlier sworn to keep. If Boaz would acquire Ruth through marriage and Naomi's property through redemption, then he could become the protector of them both. The two women could remain members of the same household, fulfilling Ruth's vow to stay with Naomi until death (1:16–17).

Boaz grasps immediately the implications of Ruth's request, understanding that she is now acting not only in her own self-interest but also out of her commitment to Naomi. He says,

> May you be blessed by the Lord, my daughter! You have acted even more faithfully than you did at first. You haven't gone after rich or poor young men. And now I'll do for you everything that you are asking. Indeed, my people—all who are at the gate—know that you are a woman of worth. (Ruth 3:10–11)

Some interpreters have understood Boaz to mean that Ruth has been even more loyal to him by proposing to marry him than she was to Naomi when she swore a lifelong commitment to her. More likely, Boaz means that Ruth has now been doubly loyal to Naomi. By choosing to marry a man who can also serve as Naomi's redeemer rather than a younger but unrelated man, Ruth has secured both of their futures with Boaz. It is this second act of loyalty to Naomi that is even greater than the first.[11]

Recognizing the depth of Ruth's commitment to Naomi, Boaz at last declares that Ruth is a "woman of worth" (3:11). His characterization of her echoes the narrator's earlier introduction of Boaz as "a man of worth" (2:1). Thus, Boaz acknowledges that Ruth, the immigrant Moabite woman, is his equal. They are suitable for one another, both being people "of worth." Boaz tells her that all the people know it, too (3:11). This claim flies in the face of the anti-immigrant rhetoric of Ezra-Nehemiah. Far from being a dangerous woman who will lead her Israelite husband astray, Ruth is a "woman of worth," a suitable partner for this Israelite man and a protector of Israelite law and custom.

Ruth and Boaz spend the night together at the threshing

floor. Just before first light, Boaz sends Ruth home, saying "No one should know that a woman came to the threshing floor" (3:14). Still dressed up and perfumed for a night on the town, Ruth sneaks home in the predawn darkness hoping no one recognizes her—the biblical version of the infamous Walk of Shame known so well to so many.

As Ruth departs, Boaz gives her six measures of barley to take with her. While it's not clear exactly how much barley this represents, it must have been a substantial amount for Ruth to carry. When Ruth arrives at home with the bounty, she tells Naomi,

> He gave me these six measures of barley, for he said to me, "Don't go away empty-handed to your mother-in-law." (3:17)

In fact, Boaz had said no such thing. Ruth misrepresents her interaction with Boaz, seemingly to indicate to Naomi that Boaz will be her provider, too. Her statement that Boaz told her not to return "empty-handed" (*reyqam*) echoes and reverses Naomi's earlier lament that "the Lord has returned me empty [*reyqam*]" (1:21), made just after they returned to Bethlehem from Moab. With her words, Ruth signals to Naomi that she will no longer be empty, and perhaps reminds her that she has never truly been empty, since Ruth has been with her all along. Naomi had sent Ruth to the threshing floor to find security for herself. Ruth has returned with security for them both.

Redemption at the Gate

All the threads of the story finally come together in a last dramatic encounter at the city gate. While Ruth and Boaz were still at the threshing floor, Boaz had told her of another redeemer more closely related to Elimelech than he (3:12). Legally, this other man seems to be the rightful redeemer of Naomi's property. Unless for some reason he refuses to buy her property, Ruth's plan will be thwarted, and Naomi will be redeemed into a different household, breaking Ruth's vow to remain with her forever.

The two men meet at the gate in front of witnesses to settle their claim. The text calls the nearer kinsman *peloni almoni* (literally "a certain someone"), akin to calling him "What's-His-Face." It is clear from the start that he is no match for Boaz.

When the men sit down, Boaz explains the situation:

> Naomi, who has returned from the field of Moab, is selling the portion of the field that belonged to our brother Elimelech. . . . If you will redeem it, redeem it; but if you won't redeem it, tell me so that I may know. (4:3–4)

This is a great deal for What's-His-Face. Since the land belongs to a widow who has no children, there will be no one to reclaim it from him in the future, at the Year of Jubilee. What's-His-Face agrees to the sale, saying, "I will redeem it" (4:4).

Just at this moment, Boaz makes an announcement that is completely unexpected by everyone involved:

> On the day that you buy the field from Naomi, I will acquire[12] Ruth the Moabite, the wife of the dead man, in order to preserve the dead man's name for his inheritance. (4:5 my translation)

This announcement is more significant than it may at first appear. First, Boaz proclaims publicly for the first time his intention to marry Ruth. While he had promised her as much in private at the threshing floor, the public affirmation by the light of day wasn't assured.

More unexpected, however, is Boaz's second announcement, which is that he will give his firstborn son to the family of Elimelech in order to preserve the dead man's legacy. Since Boaz isn't bound by the laws of levirate marriage in this case, he has no legal obligation to do this. Further, while Ruth and Naomi may have hoped for Boaz to dedicate the first child to Mahlon in order to preserve Elimelech's legacy, neither has ever asked him to do so.

Boaz's gesture is a remarkable act of faithfulness to both Naomi and Ruth. He could simply have married Ruth and left Naomi to be redeemed by What's-His-Face. Instead, he has honored not only Ruth's commitment to Naomi but also their commitment to preserving Elimelech's legacy.

Boaz's announcement also has the desired effect on What's-His-Face. Now that there is an heir in the picture to someday reclaim the land, What's-His-Face fears his own inheritance may be damaged. As a result he declares to Boaz, "You can have my right of redemption, because I'm unable to act as redeemer" (4:6). Ruth and Naomi have been redeemed into the same household. They can remain together until death parts them. Now all that remains is for a child to be born.

The Birth of a Son

Boaz's announcement at the gate has confirmed the mutual commitments of Boaz, Ruth, and Naomi, bringing them together into a new household that will provide security for them all. The events surrounding the birth of Obed then restore Ruth and Naomi to the broader community, which has been absent from the story since the first moments of their return from Moab.

When the townspeople first hear Boaz's announcement, they offer a blessing over his household, praying for fertility for Ruth:

> May the Lord grant that the woman who is coming into your household be like Rachel and Leah, both of whom built up the house of Israel. May you be fertile in Ephrathah and may you preserve a name in Bethlehem. And may your household be like the household of Perez, whom Tamar bore to Judah—through the children that the Lord will give you from this young woman. (4:11–12)

By invoking the names Rachel and Leah, two of Jacob's wives and the foremothers of eight of the tribes of Israel, the townspeople indicate that a Moabite woman may indeed build up the house of Israel and make it great again. The reference to Tamar, who was likely herself a Canaanite, confirms the point that foreigners have always been part of the foundation of Israel.

Just after the community asks God to bless Boaz and Ruth

with fertility, the narrator reports that "the Lord let her become pregnant" (4:13). Curiously, this is the one place where the book of Ruth explicitly ascribes an action to God. Previously we have heard of God's actions in the narrative only through the words of Naomi, who attributes all of the significant events of her life to God. She says that God restored food to Judah (1:6), deprived her of her family (1:13, 21), and brought Ruth to the field of Boaz (2:20). In that latter case, she sees God's hand in an event that the narrator explicitly describes as happening "by chance" (2:3). In the book as a whole, as with life, God's role in the unfolding of events remains very much a mystery.

What can't be doubted, however, is that God has entered into the story at this moment in the conception of this child, Obed. He is a child of divine favor.

When Ruth gives birth to Obed, the women of the town gather around to celebrate with her. This is the first time we have seen the women with Naomi since they first spoke with her upon her return from Moab (1:19). Obed's birth has reunited Naomi with her community. The women bless the name of God, who has given Naomi a child:

> May the Lord be blessed, who today hasn't left you without a redeemer. May his name be proclaimed in Israel. He will restore your life and sustain you in your old age. Your daughter-in-law who loves you has given birth to him. She's better for you than seven sons. (4:14–15)

The women also affirm Ruth's value to Naomi, describing her as being better than seven sons. For Naomi, who has throughout the text identified security with attachment to a male, the women's words serve as a reminder that it is ultimately Ruth's commitment to her that has restored her life. This Moabite woman has given her more security than seven sons.

The following verse reports that "Naomi took the child and held him to her breast, and she became his guardian" (4:16), at which the townspeople declare, "A son has been born to Naomi" (4:17). The family line of Elimelech has been restored. Naomi has been given new life.

Making Israel Great Again

If we return to consider the book of Ruth in the context of the anti-immigrant sentiment in the time of Ezra and Nehemiah, we can see how it challenges some of the prevailing views of its time. According to Ezra and Nehemiah, the anti-immigrant sentiment in that time focused specifically on intermarriage between Jewish men and foreign women. In both books, the people condemn Moabite women specifically (Ezra 9:1; Nehemiah 13:1), and the men of the community agree to separate from their foreign wives.

By contrast, the book of Ruth tells the story of a Moabite woman who demonstrates incredible loyalty to her Israelite mother-in-law, even in the most desperate of circumstances. Rather than remaining in Moab with her sister-in-law Orpah after the deaths of their husbands, Ruth journeys with Naomi into an uncertain future. She commits herself to the community of Israel and to Israel's God, promising to stay with Naomi for life. She learns Israelite laws and customs and uses them to gain food and favor in the fields of Boaz. She not only follows Naomi's plan to marry Boaz but also manages to secure Naomi's future in the same household. She brings Naomi back from the brink of death through her unfailing loyalty. She saves the family line of Elimelech from extinction.

In the end, Boaz and all of the people at the gate recognize her as worthy. She is a model foreigner, dedicated to the thriving of Israel and its people.

Yet, beyond her personal example, Ruth is also a significant figure in the history of Israel. The book of Ruth closes with two genealogies. In the first, the narrator tells us that Ruth's son Obed "became Jesse's father and David's grandfather" (4:17). The second, more detailed genealogy extends the family line earlier in time to Perez, the son of Judah, whose mother was the Canaanite Tamar:

> These are the generations of Perez: Perez became the father of Hezron, Hezron the father of Ram, Ram the father of Amminadab, Amminadab the father of Nahshon, Nahshon the father of Salmon, Salmon the father of Boaz, Boaz the father of Obed, Obed the father of Jesse, and Jesse the father of David. (4:18–22)

Both genealogies point to David, the greatest king of Israel, whose name provides the final punctuation of the book. The story of Ruth the Moabite has, in the end, also been the story of David, though we haven't known it until now. When Ruth is saving the family line of Elimelech, she is, in fact, saving the family line of David. Without her—and her intermarriage to Boaz—David would never have been born.

In this way, the book of Ruth provides a strong counterpoint to the anti-immigrant, anti-intermarriage voices in the time of Ezra and Nehemiah. The way to Make Israel Great Again is not to expel the foreigners from their midst. Rather, foreign women—even Moabites—have always been part of the story of Israel. Without Ruth, Naomi would not have survived. Without Ruth, David would not have been born. Without Ruth, Israel would never have been great in the first place.

Reading Ruth against the Grain

Yet, for all its presumably well-intentioned advocacy for immigrants and foreigners, the book of Ruth also—perhaps unaware—reinforces negative and even dangerous views of foreigners and immigrants that, unexamined, threaten to imperil the very people it seeks to defend.

It can be difficult for someone like me, immersed in the privileges and biases of the dominant culture, to recognize the ways that an uncritical reading of the book of Ruth can endanger immigrants and other minority populations. That's why it is imperative for us all to interpret the Bible alongside people with experiences different from our own. We can help each other see things—both in the text and in ourselves—that we might otherwise miss. With regard to the book of Ruth, for those of us who have only the experience of belonging to the dominant culture, this means paying particular attention to the interpretations of women from cultures that are minorities in the United States.

One such reader is Yolanda Norton, who approaches the

book of Ruth from a womanist perspective, foregrounding the experiences of African American women like herself.[13] She cautions us about the assimilationist impulse in the book of Ruth, familiar to her from being an African American woman in a predominately white American culture. In order to be accepted in ancient Israel, Norton observes, Ruth has had to reject her own people and the culture of her ancestors. Norton describes Ruth's famous pledge in 1:16–17 as Ruth's "assimilationist articulation," in which she "disavows herself from any Moab allegiance."[14] Once she pledges herself to Naomi, Ruth never again mentions her people or her gods. She has been absorbed completely into the new culture at the expense of her own ethnic heritage. By contrast, Ruth's sister-in-law Orpah remains committed to her own people and her own gods (1:15), thereby losing her place in the story. The choice presented by the book of Ruth is thus to be completely assimilated into the dominant culture at the cost of all connections to one's own people and culture, or to separate from Israel entirely, going back to the land of one's origins. There is no place in this story for someone who wishes to dwell in Israel while retaining a connection to her own people and culture. This choice is echoed in our own day when African Americans are accepted in the dominant culture only when they "act white," while those who remain committed to their cultural heritage may be told to "go back to Africa."

Another interpreter who can help us think more deeply about the book of Ruth is Gale Yee, an American scholar of Chinese descent. Yee describes her experience of repeatedly having to respond to the question "Where are you from?"—invariably asked by white Americans—despite being a third-generation American who grew up in Chicago.[15] Yee relates this Asian American experience of being perceived as a "perpetual foreigner" to Ruth's experience of coming to Israel. Despite having left her own people to swear loyalty to her new land, Ruth is never fully accepted by the Israelites as part of their culture. As soon as Ruth arrives in Bethlehem, the text begins to refer to her as "Ruth the Moabite" (1:22; 2:2, 6, 21; 4:5, 10), whereas in Moab it had simply called her "Ruth" (1:4, 14, 16). To the dominant culture, her ethnicity becomes an inseparable part of her name—a perpetual marker of her identity as an outsider.

Yee also relates to Ruth through the common stereotype of Asian Americans as the "model minority" in the United States. By "model minority," Yee means a minoritized person accepted in the dominant culture only to the extent that she exemplifies the "best" attributes of a well-assimilated foreigner as defined by the dominant culture. Yee describes the model minority stereotype of Asian Americans as including "respect for elders, strong family ties, intellectual giftedness, a hard-work ethic, a focus on higher education and a striving to achieve, mathematical and scientific ability, and so forth."[16] Similarly, the book of Ruth presents Ruth as embodying all the best values of a good foreigner. She is polite, deferential, well-studied in Israelite law, and respectful of Israelite customs. By upholding Ruth's value only to the extent that she models good behavior rather than affirming her value, per se, the text places all immigrants and minorities in the position of having to live up to the expectations of the dominant culture or risk being viewed as a threat.

Yet, at the same time that the text expects Ruth to perform as a model minority, it also reinforces some of the most negative stereotypes of her culture. Naomi's plan for Ruth to seduce a drunk Boaz while he is asleep at the threshing floor clearly draws on the Moabite origin story in which Lot's daughters have sex with him while he slumbers in a drunken stupor (Genesis 19:30–38). The very act that earns Ruth the high praise of being doubly loyal to Naomi requires her to live into the worst stereotypes of her people as being sexually devious and manipulative.

In all of these ways, the book of Ruth represents a danger to foreigners, immigrants, and minority populations if accepted uncritically into our own context. Any attempt to interpret Ruth for today must recognize this fundamental ambivalence of the book, encouraging its attempts to support nondominant cultures while resisting its impulses to assimilate them only in ways that benefit the dominant culture.

Reading Ruth for Today

With these warnings in mind, the core message of the book of Ruth resonates for us today as it did during the time of Ezra and Nehemiah. With the rise of anti-immigrant sentiment in the United States, it stands as a reminder that the nation as we know it would have been impossible without the contributions of immigrants who, like Ruth, committed their lives to furthering the prosperity of their new land. As the foundations of the great Davidic kingdom relied on the tenacity of a poor Moabite widow, so immigrants and foreigners built the foundations of our own nation. The book of Ruth calls us to gratitude rather than hostility, invitation rather than deportation.

Yet at the same time, the book of Ruth serves as a reminder to well-meaning members of the dominant culture to take care in the ways that we advocate for immigrants and foreigners, lest our good intentions result in more harm than good. By being alert to the ways in which the book of Ruth marks others as perpetual foreigners and model minorities, by noticing how it replicates stereotypes and biases even as it tries to undermine them, we can begin to identify such impulses in ourselves and work to undo them.

The book of Ruth also calls us to a deeper awareness of the risks undertaken by poorer immigrants, and particularly by refugees from famine and disaster, who find themselves vulnerable in an unknown culture. It beckons us to attentiveness about the perils of sex trafficking, uncompensated labor, and other forms of exploitation that threaten those who seek refuge and security on our shores.

Mostly, perhaps, the book of Ruth invites us to make the kinds of commitments that Ruth and Naomi and Boaz made to one another. Commitments that cross ethnic and religious bounds. Commitments in which each person seeks the prosperity of the other rather than focusing solely on themselves. Even more so, if we could learn to make those commitments in ways that value and embrace our cultural differences, in which Ruth could celebrate her Moabite heritage and Naomi her Israelite heritage—if we could learn to create a community in which even Orpah could be included—if we could do that, we could accomplish remarkable things.

The book of Ruth calls us to stop being afraid of one another. To break down barriers rather than building up walls of protection. To welcome strangers rather than banning their entry into the country. To uplift the talents of DACA kids and to encourage the contributions immigrants make to our communities. To elect representatives who may not look like us or believe like us but who have the community's best interests at heart. In short, the book of Ruth calls us to set aside our anxieties about each other and to live into the rich diversity that already makes America great.

Notes

1. Pilar Marrero, *Killing the American Dream: How Anti-Immigration Extremists Are Destroying the Nation* (New York: Palgrave Macmillan, 2012), 5, Kindle.

2. Marrero, *Killing the American Dream*, 220, Kindle.

3. See, for instance, Judges 3:12–30; 1 Kings 8:1, 11:1; 2 Kings 13:20–21, 24:2.

4. Tod Linafelt, *Ruth*, Berit Olam: Studies in Hebrew Narrative and Poetry (Collegeville, MN: Liturgical, 1999), 31–32.

5. Jack M. Sasson, "Ruth," in *The Literary Guide to the Bible*, ed. Robert Alter and Frank Kermode (Cambridge MA: Belknap Press of Harvard University Press, 1987), 324–25.

6. Linafelt, *Ruth*, 39.

7. Kirsten Nielsen, *Ruth: A Commentary*, The Old Testament Library (Louisville: Westminster John Knox, 1997), 69, Kindle.

8. The CEB translates "*because* you are a redeemer." However, the Hebrew *ki* can also have an asseverative sense, as I have translated it.

9. Sasson, "Ruth," 325.

10. See Jack M. Sasson, *Ruth: A New Translation with a Philological Commentary and a Formalist-Folklorist Interpretation* (Baltimore: Johns Hopkins University Press, 1979), 80–92.

11. Nielsen, *Ruth*, 76, Kindle.

12. The written Hebrew text (*ketiv*) reads "I will acquire" (*qaniyti*). The ancient Hebrew reading tradition (*qere*), followed by the Greek and Syriac, reads "You will acquire" (*qaniyta*). While both readings are plausible, contextually the first makes more sense.

13. Yolanda Norton, "Silenced Struggles for Survival: Finding Life in Death in the Book of Ruth," in *I Found God in Me: A Womanist Biblical Hermeneutics Reader*, ed. Mitzi J. Smith (Eugene, OR: Cascade, 2015), 265–79, Kindle.

14. Norton, "Silenced Struggles for Survival," 268, Kindle.

15. Gale Yee, "'She Stood in Tears amid the Alien Corn': Ruth, The Perpetual Foreigner and Model Minority," in *They Were All Together in One Place? Toward Minority Biblical Criticism*, ed. Randall C. Bailey, Tat-Siong Benny Liew, and Fernando F. Segovia (Atlanta: Society of Biblical Literature, 2009), 119–40.

16. Yee, "She Stood in Tears," 124.

3

Lamentations

On June 20, 2015, essayist and MacArthur Genius Grant recipient Ta-Nehisi Coates wrote a short Twitter essay on Black anger. This was just three days after a white supremacist had murdered nine members of Emanuel African Methodist Episcopal Church in Charleston, South Carolina, and less than a year after the killings of Eric Garner, Michael Brown, Tamir Rice, Freddie Gray, and Walter Scott. Sandra Bland would die in police custody only three weeks later. Many in the Black community took to the streets to lament and protest, demanding an end to the killings and insisting on the most basic principle that Black lives do indeed matter. Their protests were met by many—particularly in the white church—with calls for forgiveness rather than anger, reconciliation rather than protest.

In response to these calls for forgiveness and reconciliation, Coates wrote:

[I] find the idea that black anger has no real legitimacy disturbing, and ultimately racist.[1]

Feeling very weird watching coverage around Charleston. Insistence that something "positive" or "hopeful" will come out of this is bracing.[2]

Think this might be a relic of not coming up in the Christian Church. Insistence on "forgiveness" is beyond me.[3]

There never seems to be much time for anger, sorrow, even hate, for black people.[4]

The divine call for "forgiveness" and "love" is selective. And tends to fall hardest on certain people.[5]

A few weeks later, Joshua Lazard, a Christian theologian and minister at Duke University Chapel, penned an essay in which he likewise argued for the necessity of a robust Christian theology of sorrow and anger in the Black community, particularly in the face of white supremacy. Lazard wrote:

Just a day after the massacre in the historic Emanuel AME Church of Charleston, the son of one of the victims, Sharonda Coleman Singleton, offered forgiveness to Dylann Roof. As more of the victims' family members emerged to publicly forgive Roof I found myself caught between the Christian imperative to forgive that had driven them to do so, and an emotion that was irreconcilable: anger. . . . The Christian tradition doesn't uplift anger as a human experience worth having. Anger is reserved for God. The fact that the liturgical calendar doesn't have a season for anger, or include in its canon a "Righteous Indignation" Sunday, speaks to just how ingrained our anti-anger theology truly is.[6]

Together Coates and Lazard—one writing from outside the church and one from within it—raise crucial questions for the Christian community. How do we make space in our community for those who are angry, whether with God or with us? How do we respect the value of anger and protest for those who have experienced trauma, whether communal or individual? Rather than forestalling sorrow and anger with calls for forgiveness, Coates and Lazard challenge the church to make space for sorrow, anger, pain, and protest without trying to cut them short or turn them into something else.

The book of Lamentations, which reflects the humiliation and anger of the people of Jerusalem following the destruction of their city by the Babylonians in 586 BCE, provides a starting point for thinking about how to create such a space for sorrow, anger, and protest within the Christian community. Perhaps the most unflinching book of the Bible, its expression of anguish and accusation resonates wherever there is suffering, whether public or private, communal or individual. It stands within the Bible as a voice of protest against God, enfolding even the most angry and disillusioned of us into the community of faith, never correcting or silencing our lament.

The book of Lamentations contains multiple voices, each of which articulates its own experience of the community's suffering and its own theology of how to respond to it. Yet remarkably, it allows each of these voices to stand, weaving them together in a complex poetic form that holds them together as one. It recognizes that anger is necessary, that hope is difficult, and that being together in community is more important than being of one mind. It calls us to do the same.

Reading Lamentations: Setting the Stage

Lamentations gives voice to the humiliation, pain, and anger of the people following the destruction of Jerusalem by the Babylonian king Nebuchadnezzar in 586 BCE. The siege and capture of Jerusalem was no doubt a traumatic experience for the people, both physically and theologically. It shattered the community's belief that Jerusalem was the dwelling place of God and therefore indestructible, and it raised serious theological questions about how such a violent overthrow could happen to God's chosen people.

King Nebuchadnezzar and the Babylonians had laid siege to Jerusalem for eighteen months before breaching its walls. The siege had deprived the people of food, and by the end there was widespread starvation (2 Kings 25:3). The Babylonians had broken down the walls, burned the city, and destroyed the temple before carrying many of the city's elite into captivity. Lamentations is written from the perspective of those who remained in the land after Jerusalem's destruction.

According to Lamentations, the community was utterly devastated by the fall of Jerusalem. The book describes the desperation of the city this way:

> Things were better for those stabbed by the sword than for those stabbed by famine—
> those who bled away, pierced, lacking food from the field.
> The hands of loving women boiled their own children
> to become their food during the destruction of the daughter of my people. (Lamentations 4:9–10)

Whether we take this as a realistic depiction of the situation in Jerusalem or as a poetic rendering for dramatic effect, the suffering wrought by an eighteen-month siege and breach of the city walls must have been unspeakable.

Yet for all the physical suffering, the community's theological trauma may have been just as significant. An influential theology at the time, known as Zion Theology, had taught that since God's Temple was in Jerusalem—also called Zion—God would never allow the city to be destroyed. Psalm 46 provides a clear example of this theological perspective:[7]

> There is a river whose streams gladden God's city,
> the holiest dwelling of the Most High.
> God is in that city. It will never crumble.
> God will help it when morning dawns. (Psalm 46:4–5)

Yet, when the Babylonians destroyed the supposedly indestructible city and sacked the temple, it called into question everything the people had believed. Either God was not as powerful as they had imagined or God had abandoned them in their time of need. Their lives devastated, the people's theology could not address the trauma they had experienced.

In response, many turned to a theology found in Deuteronomy, which claimed that God rewards people who are obedient and punishes people who are not. A clear statement of this theology appears in Deuteronomy 30:16–18:

> If you obey the Lord your God's commandments that I'm commanding you right now by loving the Lord your God, by walking in his ways, and by keeping his commandments, his regulations, and his case laws, then you will live and thrive, and the Lord your God will bless you in the land you are entering

to possess. But if your heart turns away and you refuse to listen, and so are misled, worshipping other gods and serving them, I'm telling you right now that you will definitely die. You will not prolong your life on the fertile land that you are crossing the Jordan River to enter and possess.

According to this theology, God gives people what they deserve, reward or punishment, based on whether or not they follow God's commands.

This Reward/Punishment Theology—known in scholarly circles as the Deuteronomistic Theology because of its connection to Deuteronomy—has great explanatory force, both in the ancient world and today. On the positive side, Reward/Punishment Theology allows people to feel like they are in control of what happens to them. If you want positive outcomes, all you need to do is follow God's commands. I often see this theology having a positive effect in my work with Mercy Community Church, whose members are mostly living in shelters or on the streets. Reward/Punishment Theology gives them confidence that their lives will improve if they take responsibility by making good decisions. It helps them believe that they are suffering for a reason and that they can chart a better course for the future.

But Reward/Punishment Theology also has obvious drawbacks. This is the theology that allows the likes of Pat Robertson to blame hurricane victims for their own suffering or to warn that expressions of gay pride "will bring about the destruction of your nation. It'll bring about terrorist bombs, . . . earthquakes, tornadoes, and possibly a meteor."[8] Reward/Punishment Theology can be particularly dangerous when applied by an outsider to a situation they don't understand, as it tends toward victim blaming. It takes a detached and callous heart to tell someone who has experienced a devastating loss that their suffering is a punishment from God. No less so, it is cold and self-serving to insist that the problems in poor communities are the result of lifestyle choices while ignoring the realities of redlining, poor public education, and the school-to-prison pipeline. Reward/Punishment Theology insists that those who suffer must admit wrongdoing and repent, even if they have done nothing wrong. Reward/Punishment Theology silences protest.

Many in ancient Israel applied the Reward/Punishment Theology of Deuteronomy to the destruction of Jerusalem by Nebuchadnezzar. According to the authors of 1–2 Kings, Jerusalem was destroyed because the people were disobedient to God, who punished them by handing over the city to the Babylonians. The author of 2 Kings insists, "It was precisely because the Lord was angry with Jerusalem and Judah that he thrust them out of his presence" (2 Kings 24:20). From the perspective of Reward/Punishment Theology, the people got what they deserved.

Yet, Lamentations remains uneasy about accepting Reward/Punishment Theology as an explanation for Jerusalem's suffering. While some voices within the book affirm Reward/Punishment Theology, others challenge God and accuse God of being unreasonably angry and overly violent. While some call on the community to repent and turn toward God, others protest against God for the extent of suffering they have endured, which they insist is far beyond anything that could have been deserved. The book of Lamentations embodies the struggle among these various voices—some that accept Reward/Punishment Theology and some that protest against it—holding them together in community even as they strain against one another.

Multiple Responses to Communal Trauma

It is tempting to force Lamentations to speak with one voice—to choose a theological perspective as *the* theology of the book, either accepting or resisting Reward/Punishment Theology. Yet, a richer reading of Lamentations recognizes that the book presents multiple, competing perspectives in the voices of five different characters: a Funeral Singer, Daughter Zion, the Strong Man, a Scoffer, and the Community Voice, which speaks for the community as a whole.[9] Each voice has its own perspective on the community's devastation. Taken together, they offer a rich array of theological perspectives not only on the destruction of Jerusalem but on human suffering in general.

The Funeral Singer (Lamentations 1:1–11)

The first voice heard in Lamentations describes the devastation of the city in a detached manner, as though the suffering has not affected him directly. His speech resembles a funeral song, displaying typical elements of an ancient funeral dirge, including a traditional dirge meter, the cry "Oh no!"

('*eykhah*), a description of the misery of the city, and the theme of a reversal of fortunes. We might think of him as a professional funeral singer, just trying to do his job as he describes the devastation of the city.

The Funeral Singer speaks of Jerusalem as a personified woman, a practice common in ancient Near Eastern literature and throughout the Hebrew Bible. He depicts Jerusalem weeping over the loss of her children while her former lovers refuse to comfort her:

> Oh, no![10]
> She sits alone, the city that was once full of people.
> Once a great nation, she has become like a widow.
> Once a queen over provinces, she has become a slave.
> She weeps bitterly in the night, her tears on her cheek.
> None of her lovers comforts her. All her friends lied to her;
> they have become her enemies. (1:1–2)

As Lamentations progresses, the city of Jerusalem will come to life as a figure called Daughter Zion, a devastated woman who bears the marks of God's anger in her body. She will eventually gather herself to speak her own truth, but for now the Funeral Singer describes her suffering as an outsider, dispassionate and seemingly unaffected by her circumstances.

Using graphic imagery of sexual shaming, he describes Jerusalem being stripped and exposed before those who once admired her:

> Jerusalem has sinned greatly; therefore she has become a joke.
> All who honored her now detest her, for they've seen her naked.
> Even she groans and turns away.
> Her uncleanness shows on her clothing;

she didn't consider what would happen to her.
She's gone down shockingly; she has no comforter. (1:8–9b)

The description reflects the ancient practice of punishing a woman for sexual promiscuity by exposing her naked body in public.[11] With her "uncleanness show[ing] on her clothing" (1:9), she has become untouchable. Those she hoped would comfort her instead stay far away from her, shocked by her humiliating state.

Using the language of sexual penetration, the Funeral Singer then describes the nations "entering" into Jerusalem's temple, her most sacred of spaces:

The enemy grabbed all her treasures.
She watched the nations enter her sanctuary. (1:10)

In a shocking image, the Funeral Singer likens the looting of the Jerusalem Temple to Daughter Zion's gang rape at the hands of strangers.

What's more, in light of his Reward/Punishment Theology, the Funeral Singer suggests that Daughter Zion has deserved what she gotten. He says,

Certainly the Lord caused her grief because of her many wrong acts. (1:5)

In dramatic fashion, Lamentations illustrates how Reward/Punishment Theology can lead to victim blaming. Having been promiscuous with many lovers in the past, the Funeral Singer seems to say, Daughter Zion's sexual violation is now justified.

As modern readers, we recoil at the idea that sexual violence could ever be deserved. Yet the Reward/Punishment Theology leads the Funeral Singer to just such a conclusion. This is the danger in applying Reward/Punishment Theology, particularly for someone who has not experienced suffering directly. It can lead us to blaming hurricane victims for the loss of their homes, homeless people for the lack of affordable housing, or rape victims for the sexual aggressions of men.

Daughter Zion (Lamentations 1:12–22)

To this point in Lamentations, Daughter Zion, the city of Jerusalem personified as a woman, has remained silent as the Funeral Singer has blamed her for her own devastation. As he now begins to describe her sexual humiliation and rape, Daughter Zion can no longer hold her tongue. She speaks suddenly, beginning in verse 9c. Interrupting the Funeral Singer's description of her, she cries out,

> Lord, look at my suffering,
> my enemy has definitely triumphed! (1:9c)

Daughter Zion receives no response from God, who remains noticeably silent throughout the entire book of Lamentations. Nor does the Funeral Singer acknowledge her cry, continuing his description with detached coolness.

Yet, unwilling to be ignored, Daughter Zion finds her voice once again in 1:11, crying out again to God,

> Lord, look and take notice:
> I am most certainly despised. (1:11c)

Still receiving no response, she presses on, now crying out to anyone who will pay attention to her,

> Is this nothing to all you who pass by?
> Take notice and look:[12] Is there anything like the suffering inflicted on me,
> the grief that the Lord caused on the day of his fierce anger?
> (1:12)

Still no one seems to hear her.

Yet, we as readers can pay attention to her words. We notice that despite her intense suffering, Daughter Zion isn't crying out for help or healing. Rather, she is seeking someone to take notice of her—just to look at her. Her appeals to God are "Look [*re'eh*]!" (1:9) and "Look [*re'eh*] and take notice [*habbiytah*]!" (1:11). She makes the same appeal to the passersby: "Take notice [*habbiytu*] and look [*re'u*]!" (1:12). Often those who suffer simply wish to be seen. Before they can heal, they need someone to recognize that their pain is real. Suffering must be acknowledged.

We also notice that Daughter Zion blames her suffering not on the enemies who have attacked her but directly on God. She describes the suffering she has endured as "the grief that the Lord caused on the day of his fierce anger." Daughter Zion holds God responsible for the breaking of her walls and the invasion of her temple. God has sent her enemies to attack her. God has sent the nations to rape her.

Her description of God's attack on her is vivid and horrifying:

From above he sent fire into my bones; he trampled them.
He spread a net for my feet; he forced me backward.
He left me devastated, constantly sick. (1:13)

Moreover, Zion's suffering goes beyond the violation of her own body. She also has suffered the unspeakable loss of her children, the residents of Jerusalem:

My Lord has despised my mighty warriors.
He called a feast for me—in order to crush my young men!
My Lord has stomped on the winepress of the young woman
  Daughter Judah.
Because of all these things I'm crying. My eyes, my own eyes
  pour water
because a comforter who might encourage me is nowhere near.
My children are destroyed because the enemy was so strong.
  (1:15–16)

She is a woman completely devastated.

Contemplating her circumstances, Daughter Zion turns to the question of whether she deserves what she has received from the hands of God. She alights for a moment on Reward/ Punishment Theology, saying,

The Lord is in the right, because I disobeyed his word (1:18a)

and later claiming that God has "injured me because of all my wrong acts" (1:22b).

Yet Daughter Zion has little patience for self-blame. Instead, she moves quickly to calling for vindication against her enemies. As she remembers those who celebrated *her* destruction, she wishes for *their* destruction—she wishes for them to suffer just like she suffers:

Bring the day you have announced so that they become like
me!
Let all their evil come before you.
Then injure them like you've injured me because of all my
wrong acts;
my groans are many, my heart is sick. (1:21c–22)

If there is no one to comfort her, she at least wants someone
else to suffer. She doesn't accept what her enemies have done
to her. She is angry, and she wants vindication. Lamentations
does not correct her.

The Funeral Singer Responds (Lamentations 2:1–19)

Instead, after Daughter Zion's speech, Lamentations shifts its
attention back to the Funeral Singer (2:1–19), who seems to
have been moved by her words. He begins to speak of her
compassionately, even shedding tears on her behalf:

My eyes are worn out from weeping; my stomach is churning.
My insides are poured on the ground because the daughter of
my people is shattered,
because children and babies are fainting in the streets. (2:11)

He refers to Daughter Zion now as "the daughter of *my* people," for the first time acknowledging his connection to her.
Having listened to her words, he can no longer maintain a
dispassionate distance, untouched by the suffering of the people. He begins to acknowledge her suffering as his own.

Turning to address Daughter Zion directly, he asks,

How can I comfort you, young woman Daughter Zion?
Your hurt is as vast as the sea. Who can heal you? (2:13)

My seminary professor Kathleen O'Connor, who first showed me the beauty of Lamentations, says that this is the moment that the Funeral Singer himself becomes Daughter Zion's witness.[13] Of all those from whom Daughter Zion has sought comfort, it is finally the Funeral Singer who comforts her—not by healing her or pacifying her or telling her to forgive her attackers—but by acknowledging that she has experienced unfathomable hurt, as vast as the sea. He desires to console her but recognizes that she is inconsolable. He refrains from pat answers. He weeps on her behalf. He witnesses to her truth. He believes her.

In this way, the Funeral Singer may serve as something of a model for those of us who wish to be present for people who have experienced devastation, whether personal or communal. Rather than rushing them to resolution, we can walk alongside them. We can admit that we don't know how to comfort them. We can acknowledge that their hurt is too vast for our understanding and refrain from easy answers. We can let their suffering affect us—because we belong to each other—and we can weep on their behalf. We can believe them. We, too, can be a witness.

Also like the Funeral Singer, we can check ourselves when we begin to resort to victim blaming as an explanation for suffering. As the Funeral Singer hears Daughter Zion's story, he begins to move away from the Reward/Punishment Theology he had espoused in his first speech. Now he blames not Daughter Zion herself but the societal elites who misled her:

Your prophets gave you worthless and empty visions.
They didn't reveal your sin so as to prevent your captivity.
Instead, they showed you worthless and incorrect prophesies.
   (2:14)

He likewise accuses God of "showing no compassion" (2:17). While he had previously thought Daughter Zion deserved the punishment she received, he now distances himself from that claim. Once he has listened to her words and identified with her pain, the Funeral Singer can't blame Daughter Zion so easily.

Finally, the Funeral Singer encourages Daughter Zion to continue in her angry protest against God. He doesn't try to silence her or call on her to submit quietly. He doesn't push her toward forgiveness. Rather, he yields the floor, encouraging her to protest all the more:

Cry out to my Lord from the heart, you wall of Daughter
   Jerusalem;
make your tears run down like a flood all day and night.
Don't relax at all; don't rest your eyes a moment.
Get up and cry out at nighttime, at the start of the night shift;
pour out your heart before my Lord like water.
Lift your hands up to him for the life of your children—
the ones who are fainting from hunger on every street corner.
   (2:18–19)

Far from quieting her angry protest, the Funeral Singer joins his voice with hers. He marches with her in the streets.

Daughter Zion's Second Speech (Lamentations 2:20–22)

Emboldened by the Funeral Singer's encouragement, Daughter Zion speaks again in the final verses of Lamentations 2, now unabashedly accusing God of over-punishing her. She begins by naming the appalling reality of the violence God has committed against her:

> Lord, look and see to whom you have done this!
> Should women eat their own offspring, their own beautiful babies?
> Should priest and prophet be killed in my Lord's own sanctuary?
> Young and old alike lie on the ground in the streets;
> my young men and women fall dead by the sword. (2:20–21)

Gone from her lips is the idea that she has done something to deserve her suffering. Nothing could justify the horror of streets strewn with corpses. Nothing could justify innocent priests murdered in the sanctuary. No sin could possibly warrant women starving to the point of eating their own children. Dear God. No matter what Daughter Zion may have done—no matter what her sins may have been—she does not deserve *this*.

Now speaking directly to God as "you," Daughter Zion levels a scathing accusation:

> On the day of *your* anger, *you* killed; *you* slaughtered; *you* showed no compassion.[14]
> *You* invited—as if to a festival!—terrors on every side. (2:21c–22a)

Shaking an angry fist, Daughter Zion now protests God's wrongdoing directly to God's face. God kills—God slaughters—God lacks compassion. No god should act with such uncontrolled violence—no matter what the offense.

Finally, at the end of her speech, Daughter Zion turns

away from God altogether. After accusing God of being a compassionless destroyer, she returns to speaking of God in the third person. Whether she is speaking to us as readers or muttering to herself is unclear. But she has ceased speaking to God:

> On the day of the Lord's anger, no one escaped. Not one survived.
> The children I nurtured, that I raised myself, my enemy finished them off. (2:22)

These are the last lines Daughter Zion speaks in the book. She does not move beyond the expression of pain. She does not even seek resolution. She simply speaks her angry truth, protesting God's exercise of power and refusing to move toward hope.

Daughter Zion has no interest in forgiveness. She has no interest in self-blame. She is angry, and she wants her pain to be recognized. She is exactly the kind of figure that Ta-Nehisi Coates and Joshua Lazard want to see within the biblical tradition. She would not be in the church forgiving Dylann Roof. She would be at the South Carolina statehouse ripping the Confederate flag from its pole. She would not be quietly accepting the deaths of Freddie Gray or Sandra Bland or Michael Brown. She would be in the streets being teargassed with Black Lives Matter. She is the angry, protesting voice of a devastated community—and Lamentations does not silence her.

The Strong Man (Lamentations 3)

The third character we meet in Lamentations introduces himself in 3:1 by saying "I am the man who saw suffering by God's angry rod." The term he uses to describe himself is not the common Hebrew word for a man but rather one indicating strength or might. As a result, he is sometimes called the Strong Man, a practice I follow here. The Strong Man is hypermasculine, the kind of guy who clenches his jaw and shakes off the pain, never admitting weakness. In contrast to Daughter Zion, he accepts Reward/Punishment Theology and submits to God's authority, believing that God never gives people anything they can't handle.

Like Daughter Zion, the Strong Man has suffered. He, too, identifies God as his attacker and describes in vivid terms the pain God has inflicted upon him. He says,

> I am the man[15] who saw the suffering caused by God's angry rod.
> . . . .
> He turned his hand even against me, over and over again, all day long.
> He wore out my flesh and my skin; he broke my bones. (3:1–4)

He envisions God as an attacking animal and as an archer who uses him for target practice, driving arrows into his internal organs:

> He is a bear lurking for me, a lion in hiding.
> He took me from my path and tore me apart; he made me desolate.
> He drew back his bow, made me a shooting target for his arrows.
> He shot the arrows of his quiver into my inside parts. (3:10–13)

He likens God to a mighty warrior who has wrestled him to the ground and forced his face into the dirt:

> He crushed my teeth into the gravel;
> he pressed me down into the ashes. (3:16)

It is stark, violent imagery of personal bodily injury at the hands of an angry God.

For a time, the Strong Man seems close to giving up and losing hope. He says,

> I thought: My future is gone, as well as my hope from the Lord.
> The memory of my suffering and homelessness is bitterness and
>   poison.
> I can't help but remember and am depressed. (3:18–20)

But the Strong Man is no quitter, and he's no complainer. He grits his teeth and insists that, despite all appearances, God is always faithful:

> I call all this to mind—therefore I will wait.
> Certainly the faithful love of the Lord hasn't ended;
> certainly God's compassion isn't through!
> They are renewed every morning. Great is your faithfulness.
>   (3:21–23)

Sounding like a good Reward/Punishment theologian, the Strong Man exonerates God of all wrongdoing, reasserting his belief in God's unending faithfulness.

The Strong Man explains that God doesn't want to punish anyone. But sometimes, if we've done something wrong, God simply must. When that happens, the best thing a person can do is submit to the punishment and get through it as best they can:

It's good for a man to carry a yoke in his youth.
He should sit alone and be silent when God lays it on him.
He should put his mouth in the dirt—perhaps there is hope.
He should offer his cheek for a blow; he should be filled with
    shame.
My Lord definitely won't reject forever.
Although he has caused grief,
he will show compassion in measure with his covenant loyalty.
He definitely doesn't enjoy affliction, making humans suffer.
    (3:27–33)

Like a parent spanking a child, he says, God sometimes punishes—but God doesn't enjoy it. You can almost imagine God saying, "This hurts me more than it hurts you."

For the Strong Man, the proper response for the community is to repent:

We must search and examine our ways; we must return to the
    Lord.
We should lift up our hearts and hands to God in heaven.
We are the ones who did wrong; we rebelled. (3:40–42a)

This is a strong affirmation of Reward/Punishment Theology. If the community suffers, it is because the people have done something wrong. God wouldn't punish them if they didn't deserve it. Rather than protest, the people should repent and receive their punishment in silence. That is the only way to set things right with God.

The Strong Man's response to his suffering couldn't be more different than Daughter Zion's. Rather than crying out in protest, he calls for submission. Rather than protesting against God's excessive punishment, he puts his mouth in the dirt and accepts whatever comes. Rather than questioning his guilt, he repents. Rather than turning away from God, he clings even tighter to God in hope of a better future. Lamentations doesn't silence him, either.

The Scoffer (Lamentations 4)

Before we turn to the Community Voice, there is yet one more character in Lamentations. I call him "the Scoffer" because he takes a derisive attitude toward the community's suffering. Frankly, he's difficult to like.

Although he refers to the community as "my people" (4:3, 6, 10), the Scoffer doesn't seem to have experienced its suffering directly. Unlike Daughter Zion and the Strong Man, he never describes his own injury or loss. He has somehow managed to remain above or beyond the fray. Yet, he feels entitled to comment on the community's suffering, and he does so rather callously, as one who has no skin in the game.

The Scoffer frames his observations in economic terms rather than human ones. In his opening words, the Scoffer compares suffering children to jewels that have lost their value. He laments,

> Oh no! Gold is tarnished, even the purest gold is changed.
> Sacred jewels are scattered on every corner.
> Zion's precious children, once valued as pure gold—
> oh no!—now they are worth no more than clay pots made by a
>   potter. (4:1–2)

When he looks over Jerusalem's devastated neighborhoods, he doesn't see children in distress. He sees a loss of economic potential—a generation of young people with nothing to contribute to the economy.

The Scoffer next turns his attention to the women of Jerusalem, who are unable to feed their children because of the devastation of the city. Rather than feeling sympathy for them or being moved to help them, he describes them as wild animals incapable of nurturing their young. He says,

> Even jackals offer the breast; they nurse their young.
> But the daughter of my people has become cruel, like desert ostriches.
> The baby's tongue sticks to the roof its mouth, thirsty.
> Children ask for bread, beg for it—but there is no bread. (4:3–4)

The Scoffer doesn't mourn for mothers struggling to feed their children. Instead he derides them, declaring them unfit for motherhood. For him, these poor mothers aren't even human. They are feral animals neglecting their young.

As a believer in Reward/Punishment Theology, the Scoffer blames the people of Jerusalem for their suffering, saying,

> The Lord let loose his fury; he poured out his fierce anger.
> He started a fire in Zion; it licked up its foundations. (4:11)
> It was the Lord's presence that scattered them; he no longer notices them.
> They didn't honor the priests' presence; they didn't favor the elders. (4:16)

Unwavering in his commitment to Reward/Punishment Theology, the Scoffer shows no sign of compassion. From his perspective, God has punished them justly, and the people deserve no sympathy.

Indeed, at times the Scoffer seems almost excited by the community's suffering, describing it in graphic terms:

> Things were better for those stabbed by the sword than for
>   those stabbed by famine—
> those who bled away, pierced, lacking food from the field.
> The hands of loving women boiled their own children
> to become food during the destruction of the daughter of my
>   people. (4:9–10)

For a Reward/Punishment Theology, there is something about witnessing another's suffering that tends to confirm one's own righteousness. They suffer because they deserve it; I prosper because I am righteous. The Scoffer seems pleased by the suffering of others.

Of all the figures represented in Lamentations, the Scoffer is the one I would most like to expel. I don't want him in my community. And yet I realize that the Scoffer sounds an awful lot like the Funeral Singer did before he took the time to listen to the words of Daughter Zion. If the Funeral Singer can be converted from a detached observer to Daughter Zion's comforting witness, perhaps there is yet hope for the Scoffer—and hope for all of us—if we can but hold the community together.

The Community Voice (Lamentations 5)

Finally, the Community Voice has a chance to respond in the last chapter of the book. Speaking in the language of "we," the Community Voice represents the voice of the people of Jerusalem, speaking all together. Having now heard the voices of Daughter Zion and the Strong Man, we might expect this Community Voice to decide between them—to choose between submission to God and angry protest that refuses to submit—to decide, once and for all, how the community will handle the devastation they have experienced.

But the Community Voice refuses to take sides. It refuses to accept some voices while silencing others. Instead, it chooses its words carefully so that both Daughter Zion and the Strong Man can affirm them. It chooses to preserve the community rather than force a theological conformity. It does so by echoing ideas from both Daughter Zion and the Strong Man and by using ambiguous language that both Daughter Zion and the Strong Man can affirm, though their intentions might be quite different.

The opening petition shows how the Community Voice affirms both Daughter Zion and the Strong Man, using language characteristic of both. The Community Voice calls out to God saying,

> Lord, consider what has become of us;
> take notice [*habbiytah*] of our disgrace [*cherpah*].
> Look [*re'eh*] at it! (5:1)

The petitions to "look" and "take notice" echo the words of Daughter Zion. In her opening words in Lamentations 1, Daughter Zion had said,

> Lord, look [*re'eh*] at my suffering! (1:9)
> Lord, look [*re'eh*] and take notice [*habbiytah*]! (1:11)
> All you who pass by, take notice [*habbiytu*] and look [*re'u*]! (1:12 my translation)

When she cried out to God in 2:20, Daughter Zion had again used the same verbs:

> Lord, look [re'eh] and take notice [habbiytah] to whom you have
> done this! (2:20 my translation)

By echoing the petitions of Daughter Zion, calling on God
to "take notice" (habbiytah) and to "look" (re'eh), the Community Voice now acknowledges her voice and incorporates it
into its own speech.

At the same time, the Community Voice calls attention
specifically to its "disgrace" (cherpah), employing a favorite
word of the Strong Man, who had used it twice in his own
speeches. In 3:30, the Strong Man had commended allowing
oneself to be shamed by God saying,

> He should offer his cheek for a blow; he should be filled with
> shame [cherpah]. (3:30)

Then in 3:61, he had again called God's attention to the people's shame as evidence that God needs to act:

> Hear their jeering [cherpatam], Lord, all of their scheming
> against me. (3:61)

In this way, the Community Voice embraces the language
and concerns of the Strong Man along with those of Daughter Zion, allowing them both to hear themselves in the community's words.

For the bulk of its speech in 5:2–18, the Community Voice
then describes its situation, using images both Daughter Zion
and the Strong Man can affirm. It describes how "our property has been turned over to strangers" and how "our houses
belong to foreigners" (5:2). It describes the disruption of its
families, saying "We have become like orphans, having no

father; / our mothers are like widows" (5:3). It describes the economic exploitation by those who have taken over the city: "We drink our own water—but for a price; we gather our own wood—but pay for it" (5:4). It describes the physical violence its people have endured—its women have been raped (5:11) and its men executed (5:12) or put to forced labor (5:13).

Twice the Communal Voice refers to Reward/Punishment Theology, once affirming it like the Strong Man and once rejecting it like Daughter Zion:

The crown has fallen from our head.
We are doomed because we have sinned. (5:16)

Our fathers have sinned and are gone,
but we are burdened with their iniquities. (5:7)

By offering both perspectives, the Community Voice affirms and includes both Daughter Zion and the Strong Man without deciding between them. It embraces theological ambiguity about Reward/Punishment Theology in order to hold the community together.

In 5:19, the Community Voice next makes a turn toward God that at first sounds more like the Strong Man than Daughter Zion. It says,

But you, Lord, will rule forever;
Your throne lasts from one generation to the next. (5:19)

This turn toward God resonates with the Strong Man's view that God remains in control and will ultimately act on behalf of the community. The Community Voice, like the Strong Man, seems to entrust its future to God.

Yet the meaning of this verse is not as clear as it first seems. While the translation above seems clear enough, the Hebrew is actually quite ambiguous. One could just as reasonably translate it as

> You, Lord, sit forever.
> On your throne from generation to generation.
> (5:19 my translation)

Now rather than expressing the community's confidence in God's power to restore it, the verse rejects any hope in God's capacity or desire to respond. God will sit forever, it says, doing nothing. This sounds far more like Daughter Zion than the Strong Man.

While we could choose one of these translations, trying to settle the ambiguity in favor of either the Strong Man or Daughter Zion, it may be better to acknowledge that the meaning can't be settled. The verse simply means both things at once. As a result, both the Strong Man and Daughter Zion can speak these words together, though when they say it they mean different things entirely. The Strong Man intends these words in the first sense, as a genuine turn to God, while Daughter Zion means them in the second sense—ironically—as an accusation against God. Though their theologies are incompatible, the Strong Man and Daughter Zion can yet speak with one voice.

Throughout the final lines of its speech, the Community Voice continues to use ambiguous language that allows

Daughter Zion and the Strong Man to remain together despite their theological differences. Following the turn to God in 5:19, the Community Voice addresses a new complaint to God:

Why do you forget us continually;
why do you abandon us for such a long time? (5:20)

For the Strong Man, these words reiterate his belief in God's ultimate faithfulness despite the long delay in God's response. While God does forget, the Strong Man expects God to remember again. Yet for Daughter Zion, these same words further reinforce her previous statement that God sits continually, doing nothing. Not only does she doubt whether God will act on her behalf—now she accuses God of forgetting her altogether.

Finally, the conclusion of the Community Voice's speech in 5:21–22 can also be spoken with different meanings by Daughter Zion and the Strong Man. Lamentations 5:21 is a straightforward petition:

Return us, Lord, to yourself. Please let us return!
Give us new days, like those long ago—(5:21)

Yet the following verse, which is the final line of the book of Lamentations, again has an ambiguity that leaves its meaning unsettled.

The difficulty lies in the Hebrew expression *ki 'im* that connects 5:21 to 5:22. There are at least two reasonable possibilities for its meaning. One possibility, followed by the CEB, produces a relatively positive conclusion:

Return us, Lord, to yourself. Please let us return!
Give us new days, like those long ago—
unless you have completely rejected us,
or have become too angry with us. (5:21–22)

This translation suggests that verse 5:22 is counterfactual. That is, "Give us new days like those of long ago—*unless* you have completely rejected us (which of course you haven't)." This conclusion sounds like the Strong Man.

A second interpretation leads to the opposite conclusion—that God has in fact rejected the people:

Return us, Lord, to yourself. Please let us return!
Give us new days, like those long ago—
But rather you have completely rejected us,
and have become too angry with us.

This interpretation reflects the perspective of Daughter Zion. While God is the only one who could restore her, she has no faith that God will actually do so.

While this textual ambiguity may frustrate our desire for closure, it once again allows multiple perspectives to coexist in the same words. We can imagine the Strong Man speaking these words to insist that God will restore the community. We can imagine Daughter Zion speaking the very same words as an accusation that God has rejected the community and abandoned it altogether. Both of these voices are able to say the same words despite the fact that their theologies are so different from one another.

The poet has thus constructed the entire speech of the Community Voice so that it resists closure. It can be spoken by Daughter Zion and by the Strong Man and by everyone in between. We may imagine the Funeral Singer speaking these words—and even the Scoffer, bless his heart. The Community Voice holds all the people together during a time of devastation. It doesn't demand conformity. It doesn't silence those calling for reconciliation and forgiveness. Nor does it correct those who shake their fists in angry protest. It recognizes that no single theology, no single perspective on suffering, can hold the pain of this traumatized community.

The ABC's of Trauma

To hold all of these speaking voices together in a unified whole, Lamentations employs a second literary device that isn't apparent in most English translations. In Hebrew, each chapter is written as some variation of an alphabetic acrostic, proceeding letter by letter through the alphabet from *alef* to *tav*. In English, this would be like writing a poem in which the first line begins with A and the last line with Z.

David Slavitt has made the best attempt to render the acrostic form in English.[16] To get a sense of how the acrostic works, we can look at Slavitt's translation of the first three verses of chapter 1:

Alas, a woman, widowed, alone, the city sits
  that once was full of people and great among the nations,
  a princess among the provinces, now turned tributary.
Bereft, she weeps in the night, her bitter tears trailing down her
  cheeks.
  Of her many lovers none is left to console or comfort.
  Her friends have forsaken her now and become the friends of
  her foes.
Captive is Judah, in servitude sorely afflicted.

> A lady once, the equal of any, she is lowly now like a servant who cannot rest;
> her oppressor persecutes her in her time of torment. (1:1–3 Slavitt)

Each verse of Lamentations 1 includes three lines, with the first letter in each verse proceeding through the alphabet in sequence (Alas . . . Bereft . . . Captive). Since there are a total of twenty-two letters in the Hebrew alphabet, the chapter has twenty-two verses—one for each letter. The same pattern occurs in Lamentations 2, which likewise contains twenty-two verses of three lines each.

However, Lamentations 3 intensifies this pattern by repeating each letter of the alphabet three times, as follows:

> Afflicted am I and beset, a man whom God in his wrath has abased.
> Abused by his rod and broken, I am driven into the darkness.
> Against me, he turned his hand, and again and again.
> Bones broken, wasted, I am besieged and battered.
> Bitterness is my portion and tribulation.
> Banished, I dwell in the darkest darkness like those who are long dead.
> Chained so I cannot escape and walled in, I am a captive.
> Crying for help, I call out, but he will not hear my prayer.
> Crooked are all my paths, which he has blocked with boulders.
> (3:1–9 Slavitt)

After chapter 3, the acrostic pattern begins to fall apart. Lamentations 4 returns to the pattern of chapters 1 and 2, but with only two lines per verse rather than three. Finally, Lamentations 5 contains no acrostic at all, though it does retain a shadow of the pattern in that it has exactly twenty-two verses, the same as the number of letters in the Hebrew alphabet.

The significance of the acrostic form is open to different interpretations. Perhaps the alphabetic pattern may be a way of expressing the totality of the devastation—everything has been destroyed, from A to Z. There is nothing left. Or perhaps the alphabet gives structure to what would otherwise be an overwhelming sense of unbound grief. In danger of being overwhelmed by suffering, the poet confines it within the structure of A-B-C where it can be managed and restrained, experienced only a little bit at a time. Or perhaps the alphabet helps both the speaker and the reader to remember—to not let one thing about all that has happened slip from memory. Or perhaps it is simply an artful design, an attempt to express creativity amidst the ugliness of destruction.

Whatever we finally decide about the significance of the alphabetic acrostic, the interpretation must also account for Lamentations 5, which is not an acrostic yet retains the echo of the alphabet in its twenty-two-line structure. Perhaps it indicates that, in fact, the extent of the trauma cannot ever be named—A to Z doesn't cover it—it is beyond the capacity of speech. Or perhaps it signifies that any attempt to retain suffering within the orderly structure of the alphabet fails in the end. The devastation finally breaches the walls of the structure and overruns the poetic form.

Yet again we don't need to settle on one "correct" interpretation of the acrostic. All of these possibilities can coexist, and together they say something about the essence of trauma, which cannot be experienced all at once, lest one be completely overwhelmed. It can only be experienced in fits and starts, contained within some artificial structure that allows a person to acknowledge it without being completely inundated by it. And yet, there is also something about trauma that must be remembered. It cannot, ought not, dare not be forgotten. Spoken, acknowledged, and ultimately survived, yes. But not forgotten.

One final way of interpreting the acrostic relates to the view of multiple speaking voices I have suggested throughout this chapter. The alphabetic acrostic holds the various voices together in a unified whole, while the variations of the form reflect the diversity of their perspectives. Lamentations 1 and 2, which have the same three-line structure, are the chapters shared by the Funeral Singer and Daughter Zion. In Lamentations 3, the insistent voice of the Strong Man takes shape within the intensified acrostic in triplicate. Lamentations 4 presents the view of the Scoffer in a truncated, two-line form. Finally, Lamentations 5 preserves the twenty-two verse structure, shared in various ways by all the voices, but doesn't attempt to conform them to one specific alphabetic structure.

In this way, the acrostic form ties together the voices from all across the community—the Funeral Singer, Daughter Zion, the Strong Man, the Scoffer, and the Community Voice. They recognizably belong to each other, even as they strain against one another. When they doubt whether or not they belong together, the acrostic insists that they do. Though they are not the same, they share a common connection. Without any one of them, the whole would be incomplete.

Reading Lamentations Today

For contemporary readers, Lamentations insists that we, too, all belong together. Those who have experienced trauma and those who walk alongside them, united by our common community and by our common humanity—even if not by our theological conformity.

For those who have experienced trauma—whether personal loss or communal tragedy—Lamentations offers both Daughter Zion and the Strong Man, whose divergent responses to devastating loss make space for a wide range of faithful responses from us. For the Strong Man, hope remains at the horizon of tragedy. In the darkness, he hopes for the dawn, believing that day will break and that God will restore him at any moment. Daughter Zion, by contrast, has no use for hope. She is devastated, humiliated, and angry. She has no faith that God will restore her, and she protests loudly against both God and those who have injured her. She demands to have her suffering acknowledged, to know that others see and recognize the devastation of her community and the wounds of her body. Embracing her anger, she refuses to move toward hope.

For those who have not experienced trauma directly, Lamentations offers the Funeral Singer as a reminder that we, too, can be witnesses to the suffering of others by listening and by allowing ourselves to be moved and changed by their experiences. It reminds us that we can create space for voices of protest and encourage the speaking of truth to power. Lamentations also offers us the Scoffer, perhaps as a reminder of who we don't want to be. Yet even the Scoffer is allowed to remain in the community, holding out the hope that he, too, might hear and be changed.

In this way, Lamentations reminds us that we all belong together, that we all belong to each other—that one person's suffering is all of our suffering. It reminds us that our stories are knit together in a great acrostic tapestry of faith that holds our pain and sorrow, that gives us words to name it, and that will not allow us to forget. And in all our diversity—of experience, of theology—Lamentations reminds us that we can give each other the space to speak, the space to breathe, the space to protest—without losing our common voice and without forgetting our common humanity.

Notes

1. Ta-Nehisi Coates (@tanehisicoates), Twitter, June 20, 2015, 10:56 p.m., http://tinyurl.com/yctaqfya.

2. Coates, Twitter, June 21, 2015, 8:17 a.m., http://tinyurl.com/yao2omto.

3. Coates, Twitter, June 21, 2015, 8:18 a.m., http://tinyurl.com/y8clx63l.

4. Coates, Twitter, June 21, 2015, 8:20 a.m., http://tinyurl.com/ybewxy58.

5. Coates, Twitter, June 21, 2015, 8:22 a.m., http://tinyurl.com/y7hmqbjy.

6. Joshua L. Lazard, "A Theology of Anger: Forgiveness for White

Supremacy Derails Action and Alienates Young Black Activists," Religion Dispatches, July 6, 2015, http://tinyurl.com/y8sp6ndw.

7. See also Psalms 48, 76, and 125.

8. Thomas B. Edsell, "Forecasting Havoc for Orlando," *The Washington Post*, June 10, 1998, http://tinyurl.com/y6uws223.

9. While most scholars now recognize multiple voices in Lamentations, they vary in terms of the number and identity of voices. The foundational analysis is William F. Lanahan, "The Speaking Voice in the Book of Lamentations," *Journal of Biblical Literature* 93, no. 1 (1974): 41–49.

10. The Hebrew *'eykhah* is difficult to translate effectively. It is, in essence, an exclamation of pity, sometimes translated "Alas!" (NJPS) or "How!" (NRSV). We should imagine a gasp of horror and disbelief as the speaker utters this word.

11. See Hosea 2:3; Ezekiel 16:35–39, 23:29.

12. I have adapted the CEB translation to capture the repetition of terms.

13. Kathleen M. O'Connor, *Lamentations and the Tears of the World* (Maryknoll, NY: Orbis, 2002), 39.

14. My translation. The CEB translates "you killed, you slaughtered, showing no compassion," obscuring the third direct accusation.

15. The CEB's "someone" obscures the gender of the speaker.

16. David R. Slavitt, *The Book of Lamentations: A Meditation and Translation* (Baltimore, MD: Johns Hopkins University Press, 2001).

4

Ecclesiastes

The fear of death is a powerful force in human life. It motivates us to achieve great accomplishments, and it drives us to commit horrible atrocities. Over the past thirty years, researchers in a field of social psychology known as Terror Management Theory (TMT) have demonstrated that protecting ourselves from death anxiety motivates much of human life, from the careers we choose to the wars we wage.

In their groundbreaking book *The Worm at the Core: On the Role of Death in Life*, leading TMT researchers Sheldon Solomon, Jeff Greenberg, and Solomon Pyszczynski argue that

> over the course of human history, the terror of death has guided the development of art, religion, language, economics, and science. It raised the pyramids in Egypt and razed the Twin Towers in Manhattan. It contributes to conflicts around the globe. At a more personal level, recognition of our mortality leads us to love fancy cars, tan ourselves to a crisp, max out our credit cards, drive like lunatics, itch for a fight with a perceived enemy, and crave fame, however ephemeral, even if we have

to drink yak urine on *Survivor* to get it. . . . Awareness of the inevitability of death could easily contribute to our own extinction if we don't change how we deal with it.[1]

Anxiety about death drives us in ways that we can only begin to understand.

We live our lives in the tense space between our desire to live and the awareness that we will someday die. As a result, we are driven to conceive of our lives as having some kind of significance that will allow us to remain connected with life even after we die. Some of us may invest ourselves in religion and believe in a literal afterlife in heaven. Others may strive for significance by writing that great American novel that will be read long after we die. Some may hope to found a company that will change the world or make enough money to endow a foundation to carry on our life's work. Others may fight to preserve American values around the globe or join the Peace Corps to make a difference in the lives of those less fortunate. Some pursue fame as an actor or musician. Others make viral cat videos. But all of us seek ways to remain significant in ways that will leave a mark on the world after we're gone.

This is all well and good until something calls into question the pursuits we have undertaken in that effort. When we fail to get the promotion at work and realize we will never make enough money to leave a foundation, we may find ourselves overwhelmed by the sense that our life has no meaning. When we get a rejection slip from a book publisher or fail to get a callback for an audition, we realize that we will never achieve the sort of fame that will make people remember us. When we reach the end of our lives and look back over it all, we may realize we've spent our time in the pursuit of things that simply didn't matter.

In the worst case, unexamined death anxiety can turn to violence. When we encounter a person or a culture that believes a different religion is the one true religion, it threatens our sense of significance and our claim to symbolic immortality. When we encounter someone who believes socialism is superior to capitalism or that the United States has done more harm than good in the world, it may call into question the most fundamental commitments that give our lives meaning and that protect us against being overwhelmed by anxiety about death. According to TMT research, we are so loath to experience this kind of death anxiety that our instinct is to eliminate anyone who threatens our fundamental beliefs, whether by converting them to our own views or by blocking them on Facebook—or, if we have access to an army or a nuclear bomb, by wiping them off the face of the earth.

If it is indeed the case that our denial of death is at the root of both human misery and human violence, Ecclesiastes may be the most important biblical book of all. It invites us into an honest conversation about death's inevitability, reminding us of the futility of all our efforts to secure symbolic immortality. It denies any possibility of death transcendence, whether literal or symbolic, forcing us to grapple with our own finitude. It invites us to face the fact of death simply and authentically, reflecting on what it means to live a meaningful life when we know that death awaits us in the end.

Reading Ecclesiastes: Setting the Stage

Traditionally, Ecclesiastes has been attributed to King Solomon. Yet both the style of the Hebrew and the cultural references in the book point to a time much later than Solomon—in the periods of either Persian (538–331 BCE) or Greek (331–164 BCE) rule. Most scholars date the book to the early Greek period, sometime around 280 BCE, nearly seven centuries after the time of Solomon.

In fact, Ecclesiastes never actually uses the name of Solomon with reference to the author. The main speaker in the book uses the Hebrew pseudonym "Qohelet," which literally means "(the) Gatherer" or "(the) Assembler." The King James Version translates Qohelet as "the Preacher," referring to one who leads an assembly of believers. Other translations use "the Teacher," as one who leads an assembly of students. I myself will simply call Qohelet "the Gatherer." Whatever else we may say about him, we know that he is one who gathers observations about the world, collects wisdom sayings and proverbs, and interprets them for us.

Finally, we should note that the Gatherer is not, in fact, the only speaker in the book. While he speaks for the vast majority of the book, from Ecclesiastes 1:2–12:8, there is also a frame narrator who speaks in 1:1 and 12:9–14 and makes occasional insertions throughout the book (1:2; 7:27; 12:8). We can recognize the frame narrator because he talks *about* the Gatherer, whereas in the rest of the book the Gatherer speaks for himself. For instance, the frame narrator introduces the book by saying "The words of the Gatherer" (1:1) and summarizes the Gatherer's teachings in 12:9–14.

We'll focus on the words of the Gatherer, whom I take to be the primary voice in the book, leaving aside the frame narrator for another time.

The Gatherer's Quest for Death Transcendence

The Gatherer's first words in Ecclesiastes 1:2 have become one of the book's most well-known sayings. The statement serves as a kind of theme for the book as a whole, repeated by the Gatherer some thirty-eight times.[2] In the traditional King James translation, the Gatherer says:

Vanity of vanities . . . vanity of vanities; all is vanity. (1:2 KJV)

Vanity here doesn't refer to looking in the mirror too much or thinking this song is about you (don't you?) but rather to working hard at something to no avail (as in "all her efforts were in vain"). The CEB translation, which I am using in this book, renders the phrase as "everything is pointless."

However, the Hebrew term *hevel* that the Gatherer uses actually has the root meaning of "vapor" or "breath," so that what the Gatherer actually says is something like "everything is only vapor" or "everything is merely breath." Life is like the mist that forms when you exhale on a cold winter's night. It dissipates quickly. You can't grasp it or hold onto it. It is there—and then it is gone.

The observation that everything is fleeting leads the Gatherer to the question that will frame his thinking throughout the entire book. He asks,

> What do people gain from all the work
> that they work so hard at under the sun? (1:3)

The Hebrew word "gain" (*yitron*) is an economic term that refers to the net profit of a business once all the expenses have been accounted for. The Gatherer conceives of a person's life as a balance sheet, asking what profit will be left over when all is said and done. In the terms of TMT, the Gatherer wants to know what about a person continues on after death. He wants to know in what way a person can achieve symbolic immortality.

Of course, the Gatherer has already given us his answer, which he will repeat again and again throughout the book: Everything is vanity. Everything is pointless. Everything is a vapor that disappears like a breath in the night. When a person dies, nothing remains.

The Futility of Human Striving

To test his claim, the Gatherer undertakes a thought experiment. He imagines himself to be a great king—probably King Solomon—asking whether even someone as great as he could achieve any death-transcending gain in life. As Solomon, the Gatherer sets out to do the things that kings do to secure a lasting legacy for themselves. He plants lush gardens and installs elaborate pools (2:5). He acquires servants, cattle, and sheep (2:8), amassing great wealth and "every human luxury" until he becomes "greater than all who preceded me in Jerusalem" (2:9). Then, still imagining himself as Solomon—the wisest (1:16) and wealthiest (2:9) person ever to live in Jerusalem—the Gatherer stands back to see what he has accomplished.

Yet when he looks over all he has done, all he has built, all he has acquired, all he has achieved, he concludes,

> It was pointless [*hevel*]—a chasing after the wind.
> Nothing is to be gained [*yitron*] under the sun. (2:11)

A few verses later, the Gatherer explains how he has reached this conclusion. He says,

> I thought to myself, What happens to the fool will also happen to me. So why have I been so very wise? I said to myself, This too is pointless. There is no eternal memory of the wise any more than the foolish, because everyone is forgotten before long. How can the wise die just like the fool? (2:15–16)

The Gatherer realizes that death happens to everyone in the same way—the wise person dies exactly the same kind of death as the fool. Neither one leaves anything behind to preserve their legacy among the living. Neither one achieves any kind of symbolic immortality. People will eventually forget you. The great gardens you plant will be overtaken by weeds. The palaces you construct will crumble. The books you write will gather dust in a forgotten library. Your kids will be idiots who waste the inheritance you leave them (2:18–21). Nothing you do will preserve your legacy after death—whether wise or fool, it will eventually be as though you had never been.

This conclusion stands in contrast to what the Gatherer's worldview has taught him. According to Proverbs, wisdom and righteousness do have benefits that preserve the significance of a person's life beyond death. The clearest example is found in Proverbs 10:7:

> The memory of the righteous is a blessing,
> but the name of the wicked rots. (10:7)

According to this saying, following the way of life prescribed by Proverbs has death-transcending benefits, while failing to do so results in your total annihilation after death.[3] A wise person will be remembered and her memory will continue to bless the living whenever she is called to mind. By contrast, the wicked person dies and is forgotten, his name rotting in the grave along with him. Other proverbs say that the righteous will live on in their children[4] and in their students,[5] while only the wicked will be utterly erased.

The Gatherer, by contrast, rejects the distinction between the wise and the foolish, at least at the level of death transcendence. Death does not distinguish between the wise and the foolish, allowing some to live on while others are completely erased. Rather, the Gatherer sees that in the end we are all the same, completely erased by time and forgetfulness.

Nor does the Gatherer have confidence that God will distinguish between the righteous and the wicked by rewarding the righteous with a literal afterlife in some great beyond. At one point, the Gatherer muses on the possibility of a literal life after death. He says,

> I also thought, Where human beings are concerned, God tests them to show them that they are but animals because human beings and animals share the same fate. One dies just like the other—both have the same life-breath. Humans are no better off than animals because everything is pointless.
>
> > All go to the same place;
> > all are from the dust;
> > all return to dust.
>
> Who knows if a human being's life-breath rises upward while an animal's life-breath descends into the earth? (3:18–21)

Paraphrasing Genesis 3:19, the Gatherer claims that every creature, both human and animal, dies in the same way, returning to the dust from which they came. Since both humans and animals have the same "life-breath" (3:19), there is no reason to think that the breath of one rises to heaven while the other descends to the earth (3:21). Humans die in the same ways as animals, he believes. There is no life after death.

These observations about the impossibility of surviving death in any way—literal or symbolic—run the Gatherer headlong into death's finality. He encounters death without symbolic buffers, without the protection of a worldview that promises that he will remain significant after he dies. Facing death in this way, he says,

> I hated life, because the things that happen under the sun were troublesome to me. Definitely, everything is pointless—just wind chasing. (2:17)

Realizing that all we have to look forward to is dying and being forgotten—that there is no way to insure our significance beyond death—the Gatherer despairs over the purpose of life. If you are seeking symbolic immortality, you might as well be chasing the wind.

The Injustices of Life

While the Gatherer concludes that there is nothing he can do to achieve symbolic immortality, he might at least take some comfort in the possibility that his efforts could bring him success and security during his own lifetime. Again, Proverbs has promised him as much. It says,

> No harm happens to the righteous,
> but the wicked receive their fill of trouble. (Proverbs 12:21)

and

> The righteous eat their fill,
> but the wicked have empty stomachs. (Proverbs 13:25)

and

> Great treasure is in the house of the righteous,
> but the gain of the wicked brings trouble. (Proverbs 15:6)

According to Proverbs, hard work and righteous living pay off.

But when the Gatherer examines the world around him, he sees that there is no relationship between a person's actions and the outcomes of their life. He says,

I have seen everything in my pointless lifetime: the righteous person may die in spite of their righteousness; then again, the wicked may live long in spite of their wickedness. (Ecclesiastes 7:15)

Indeed, people often seem to get the *opposite* of what they deserve:

Here's another thing that happens on earth that is pointless: the righteous get what the wicked deserve, and the wicked get what the righteous deserve. I say that this too is pointless. (8:14)

At times, the Gatherer seems to question whether there is any place for righteousness at all:

I saw something else under the sun: in the place of justice, there was wickedness; and in the place of what was right, there was wickedness again! (3:16)

Everywhere he turns there is wickedness. Bad people prosper while good people suffer.

As the Gatherer observes the injustice and oppression that takes place in the world, he concludes that living in such a world may actually be worse than death. He says,

I declare that the dead, who have already died, are more fortunate than the living, who are still alive. But happier than both are those who have never existed, who haven't witnessed the terrible things that happen under the sun. (4:2–4)

While he had previously despaired over the inevitability of death, the Gatherer now longs for death as a relief from the pain and injustice of life. He wishes for a world that functions the way it is supposed to, in which the righteous are rewarded and the wicked punished. But since the world is topsy-turvy, the Gatherer would rather be dead than live through the sound and fury of life. The Gatherer is caught in the grip of despair.

The Gatherer's View of God

To this point, I have focused on the Gatherer's views of life "under the sun," without much reference to God. Yet for the Gatherer, both the injustices of life and the finality of death are deeply tied to his view of God. While he struggles with the nature of life and death, at a deeper level the Gatherer wrestles with the very foundations of the religious worldview he has been taught.

A good place to begin thinking about the Gatherer's view of God is his description of how one should approach God in the temple, which appears in 5:1–7. The Gatherer warns,

> Watch your steps when you go to God's house. It's more acceptable to listen than to offer the fool's sacrifice—they have no idea that they're acting wrongly. Don't be quick with your mouth or say anything hastily before God, because God is in heaven, but you are on earth. Therefore, let your words be few. (5:1–2)

There is some irony in the Gatherer's instruction to "watch your steps when you go to God's house" (5:1). Elsewhere in the Bible, it is God who watches over the worshipper's steps, offering protection from danger (see, for example, Psalms 91:11–12 and 121:3). Here, by contrast, it is God who is dangerous and the worshipper who must be cautious in guarding their own steps.[6] The Gatherer's God is not to be trifled with. Saying too much, or saying the wrong thing, may draw a divine rebuke.

The Gatherer continues by saying,

> When you make a promise to God, fulfill it without delay because God has no pleasure in fools. Fulfill what you promise. Better not to make a promise than to make a promise without fulfilling it. Don't let your mouth make a sinner of you, and don't say to the messenger: "It was a mistake!" Otherwise, God may become angry at such talk and destroy what you have accomplished.
>
> > Remember:
> > When dreams multiply,
> > so do pointless thoughts and excessive speech.
> > Therefore, fear God. (5:4–7)

The Gatherer's basic posture before God is "fear" (5:7). While the Hebrew word *yara'* can mean "to be reverent," as it does often in Proverbs (e.g., Proverbs 3:7, 24:21), the Gatherer actually seems to think we should genuinely be afraid of God. He doesn't speak of the good things God will do for you if you go to the temple, only of the dangers that lurk there. Saying the wrong thing, saying too much, or attracting the wrong kind of attention may result in God destroying everything you have done. It's better to lie low and hope God doesn't notice you.

The Gatherer does believe that God can be benevolent at times, as he remarks on God blessing people with good things. For instance, the Gatherer says,

> Whenever God gives people wealth and riches and enables them to enjoy it, to accept their place in the world and to find pleasure in their hard work—all this is God's gift. (5:19)

In this case, God has given certain people wealth and riches, along with the capacity to enjoy them. However, just a few verses later, the Gatherer describes a different situation:

> God may give some people plenty of wealth, riches, and glory so that they lack nothing they desire. But God doesn't enable them to enjoy it; instead, a stranger enjoys it. This is pointless and a sickening tragedy. (6:2)

In this second case, God has given people wealth, riches, and glory but has withheld their capacity to enjoy it. Instead a "stranger" enjoys it. No reason is given for why God has given one set of people the capacity to enjoy and withheld it from the other. There is no suggestion that one group was righteous and the other wicked, or that one group somehow deserved to enjoy their wealth and the other didn't. Rather, God has simply given some people the capacity to enjoy and withheld it from others.

The Gatherer concludes that human beings ultimately have no way of knowing or understanding what God is doing in the world—why God blesses some of us and curses others. He says,

> I observed all the work of God—that no one can grasp what happens under the sun. Those who strive to know can't grasp it. Even the wise who are set on knowing are unable to grasp it. (8:17)

No amount of religious instruction or theological reflection will ever make sense of it. We simply can't understand what God is up to.

What's more, the Gatherer thinks that even if we *could*

somehow understand God's actions toward us (which we can't), there would still be nothing we could do to influence them. He says,

> Whatever happens has already been designated, and human beings are fully known. They can't contend with one who is stronger than they are. . . . Who knows what's good for human beings during life, during their brief pointless life, which will pass away like a shadow? Who can say what the future holds for people under the sun? (6:10–12)

God has already decided what to do with us, and there's nothing we can do about it. As a friend of mine says, "God gonna God."[7] One must simply keep one's head down, try not to attract too much attention, and accept whatever fate God decides to give.

Letting Go of Illusions

By this point, the Gatherer has thoroughly shattered the illusions that protect us from the apparent meaninglessness of lives lived in the face of inevitable death. He has left us with an unfiltered view of the pointlessness of our efforts to secure significance through the successes we achieve in life. He has forced us to face the reality that no matter how hard we work to make a future for ourselves and our children, our lives can at any moment be upended by a stock market crash, an automobile accident, or a debilitating illness. He has even deprived us of a comforting God just waiting to set everything straight, reminding us that as often as not God seems to reward the wicked while the righteous die of cancer at the age of thirty-five.

How can a person even begin to live in such a world?

For the Gatherer, the first step is to name the illusions we live by for what they are: breath, mist, vapor, insubstantial *hevel*. We have already seen how the Gatherer examines all of the measures of kingly success—houses, vineyards, gardens, servants, slaves, herds, treasures, luxuries—and concludes that they are worth nothing. They cannot secure one against the coming annihilation of death.

Nor can wealth and riches ever bring a person satisfaction. The Gatherer points out that as we feed our appetites for wealth and luxury, we end up desiring wealth and luxury all the more. He says,

> The money lover isn't satisfied with money; neither is the lover of wealth satisfied with income. This too is pointless. When good things flow, so do those who consume them. But what do owners benefit from such goods, except to feast their eyes on them? Sweet is the worker's sleep, whether there's a lot or a little to eat; but the excess of the wealthy won't let them sleep. (5:10–12)

The Gatherer sees that people work themselves to death in the pursuit of things that are ultimately pointless. He observes people who "work hard and become good at what they do only out of mutual envy" (4:4). These people lose sleep over their latest business ventures, fret over their savings, compare themselves to the Joneses—all in pursuit of things that will never satisfy them. It is better, he says, to be content with the fruits of a good day's labor, whether in plenty or in want.

Further, the Gatherer reminds us that the world is fundamentally unpredictable. No matter how carefully we save and prepare, wealth can be lost as quickly as it comes. He tells the story of a person who has stored up all of their wealth but never has a chance to enjoy it:

> I have seen a sickening tragedy under the sun: people hoard their wealth to their own detriment. Then that wealth is lost in a bad business venture so that when they have children, they are left with nothing. Just as they came from their mother's womb naked, so they'll return, ending up just like they started. All their hard work produces nothing—nothing they can take with them. This too is a sickening tragedy; they must pass on just as they arrived. What then do they gain from working so hard for wind? What's more they constantly eat in darkness, with much aggravation, grief, and anger. (5:13–17)

In the first half of this passage, the Gatherer imagines a person who has lost their life savings in a bad business venture. While they counted on their wealth to provide security for the future, they now have nothing—they can't feed their children, let alone leave them an inheritance. Further, the person has spent their life working too hard, coming home for dinner after sunset, wasting all their days in aggravation, grief, and anger—all for something that could not save them from life's unpredictable turns.

While this scenario is terrible, the Gatherer thinks an even worse situation is a person who actually manages to achieve wealth and success but is never able to appreciate what they have. He says,

> Some people may have one hundred children and live a long life. But no matter how long they live, if they aren't content

with life's good things, I say that even a stillborn child with no grave is better off than they are. Because that child arrives pointlessly, then passes away in darkness. Darkness covers its name. It hasn't seen the sun or experienced anything. But it has more peace than those who lived a thousand years twice over but don't enjoy life's good things. Isn't everyone headed to the same destination? (6:3–6)

While these people achieve their dreams, receiving everything life has to offer—wealth, children, and a healthy long life—they are so caught up in the pursuit of their goals that they can never truly enjoy them. The Gatherer compares people who live this way to a stillborn child, arguing that the stillborn has the better part of the deal. It is better not to have lived at all than to have spent a lifetime fretting about wealth and status when in the end none of it matters.

However, it isn't just the pursuit of wealth that is an illusion. It is the pursuit of *all* culturally prescribed modes of "success"—the measures by which we judge ourselves to be better than another person. TMT researchers Solomon, Greenberg, and Pyszczynski describe the culturally constructed nature of success as follows:

> For the Dinka of Sudan, the man who owns the largest herd of long-horned cattle is the most highly regarded. In the Trobriand Islands, a man's worth is measured by the size of the pyramid of yams he builds in front of his sister's house and leaves to rot. For many Canadians, the man who best uses his stick to slap rubber pucks into nets guarded by masked opponents is considered a national hero.[8]

We all have arbitrary measures of our own value that, upon examination, dissipate like so much breath. My college students already come out of high school wanting to "be somebody." They feel pressure to achieve success in all of the ways our culture prescribes, whether by making money, rising to positions of influence, or having a "prestige" career as a doctor or lawyer. Others of us measure success by the car we drive or the vacations we take or the balance of our 401(k). Even as I sit here writing this book, I hope that I will be successful—that you will think well of me, that I will gain Twitter followers, that I may get a good review in *Christian Century* or an invitation to speak at the Wild Goose Festival. We all want to matter.

Yet, the Gatherer reminds us that all our pursuits are ultimately only illusory measures of success. They can't protect us from death or even from the vicissitudes of life. They can't secure our futures or satisfy our appetite for more. They are, the Gatherer says, utterly pointless—so much chasing of the wind.

Living in the Face of Death

So far, Ecclesiastes is a bit of a downer. Maybe the Gatherer isn't the guy you invite to a party. He would probably just sit in the corner, wearing black, smoking a cigarette, and talking about Camus.

But the *reason* the Gatherer is such a downer is because he makes us face the possibility that the things we are pursuing in life are ultimately worthless. They can't do what we want them to do for us, which is to make us significant in the face of death. He has exposed our anxiety about death and the futility of life, and so far he has given us nothing in return.

Only now, once he has stripped away the illusions of our symbolic immortality projects, does the Gatherer begin to seek ways of living meaningfully in the face of inescapable death. In 2:24, the Gatherer first finds a sliver of hope in a life lived in death's shadow. Shortly after saying that he hates life because the wise and the fool die in the same way (2:15–17), the Gatherer offers this advice:

> There's nothing better for human beings than to eat, drink, and experience pleasure in their hard work. (2:24a)

Elsewhere he says,

> I know that there's nothing better for them but to enjoy them-selves and do what's good while they live. Moreover, this is the gift of God: that all people should eat, and drink, and enjoy the results of their hard work. (3:12–13)

And again,

> I commend enjoyment because there's nothing better for peo-ple to do under the sun but to eat, drink, and be glad. This is what will accompany them in their hard work, during the life-time that God gives under the sun. (8:15)

When all else is stripped away, the Gatherer finds good in the most mundane things in life—eating good food, drinking good wine, and enjoying what you do. This is a far cry from the frantic building and acquiring he has pursued elsewhere in the book. The good life is not about amassing wealth or pursuing significance but simply enjoying the things we have the best we can.

The Gatherer suggests that the purpose of work is simply

to enjoy working. We should seek jobs that bring us satisfaction rather than ones we think will gain us respect and admiration or earn us a great deal of money. Nor should we fall into the trap of spending our lives in pursuit of a perfect job that will completely fulfill us. It doesn't exist. Rather, the Gatherer thinks we should seek the joy in whatever work we find to do, whether writing books or caring for patients or sweeping floors. Your work won't make you significant in the face of death—but it can bring you joy in the present moment.

However, even the advice to enjoy life has to be moderated. The Gatherer recognizes that we can't find joy in life just because we decide to. Life is hard and full of disappointments. Rather, the Gatherer tells us, it is God who gives the capacity for enjoyment and God who can take it away. He advises,

> When times are good, enjoy the good; when times are bad, consider: God has made the former as well as the latter so that people can't discover anything that will come to be after them. (7:13–14)

Since we can't know what lies ahead of us, whether good times or bad, and we can't understand what God is doing in the world, we simply have to take life as it comes. The Gatherer tells us to enjoy life when we can, realizing that the good times can't last forever. When the bad times do come—and inevitably they will—we simply remember that we've had some good times, too, and we try to be grateful for those.

As the Gatherer moderates his expectations, he also shifts

his language about what a person can hope to achieve in life. While in the beginning (1:3) the Gatherer had sought a "gain" (*yitron*) for all his toil—a balance on the balance sheet at the end of his life—over the course of the book he introduces the more modest quest of finding a "share" (*cheleq*) in life. In 3:22 he says,

> So I perceived that there was nothing better for human beings but to enjoy what they do because that's their share[9] in life. (3:22 CEB adapted)

He uses the same term again in 5:18:

> This is the one good thing I've seen: it's appropriate for people to eat, drink, and find enjoyment in all their hard work under the sun during the brief life time that God gives them because that's their share in life. (5:18 CEB adapted)

Like *gain*, a *share* is an economic term. However, while *gain* refers to a permanent profit left over after the books are closed, a *share* has only temporary value that can't be carried over. It's kind of like a gift card with a very close expiration date. In terms of the Gatherer's metaphor for life, a *share* has no lasting value that shows up on the books at the end of life. In fact, it expires almost as soon it is received. However, it does have value in the present moment, however fleeting.

Because the Gatherer thinks that finding a death-transcending gain is impossible, he commends appreciating the short-term shares whenever we can find them. Enjoying the good things in the present moment is the greatest possible good a person can achieve.

The Seasons of Life

The Gatherer's emphasis on accepting the present moment for what it is—and enjoying it the best you can—forms the basis of one of the most well-known passages of Ecclesiastes, immortalized for better or for worse in The Byrds' 1965 song "Turn, Turn, Turn." (Now you can't get that song out of your head, can you?)

In Ecclesiastes 3:1–8, the Gatherer describes life as a series of seasons:

> There's a season for everything
> and a time for every matter under the heavens:
> a time for giving birth and a time for dying,
> a time for planting and a time for uprooting what was planted,
> a time for killing and a time for healing,
> a time for tearing down and a time for building up,
> a time for crying and a time for laughing,
> a time for mourning and a time for dancing,
> a time for throwing stones and a time for gathering stones,
> a time for embracing and a time for avoiding embraces,
> a time for searching and a time for losing,
> a time for keeping and a time for throwing away,
> a time for tearing and a time for repairing,
> a time for keeping silent and a time for speaking,
> a time for loving and a time for hating,
> a time for war and a time for peace. (3:1–8)

The poem encapsulates some of the most important aspects of human life: birth and death, killing and healing, embracing and separating, love and hate, war and peace.

For the Gatherer, each of these things has its proper time and its appropriate place in life (3:1). Every life passes through these seasons, and we shouldn't expect it to be otherwise. We will celebrate births and mourn deaths. We will find new relationships and let go of old ones. We will dance in celebration and mourn in lamentation. This is all to be expected and cannot be avoided.

Because life moves in seasons, there is also no experience that will last forever. In one sense this is good news. When we are living through something difficult, we know that a better time will come. Dawn eventually breaks on even the darkest night of the soul. Yet, this poem also insists that the good times can't last forever, either. Laughing will eventually turn into mourning, and peacetime will eventually revert back to war (sorry, Byrds). We can create enormous anxiety for ourselves by trying to hang on to something good beyond its time, knowing that it can't last. Enjoy the moment, says the Gatherer. What will come will come.

Yet there is another aspect of this poem that is easy to miss. Though we tend to read 3:1–8 as though it stands alone, the Gatherer connects it to the following verse, in which he asks a familiar question:

What do workers gain from all their hard work? (3:9)

The answer, as we know by now, is *nothing*. There is no possibility of gain in life.

But when the Gatherer asks this question at this particular moment, he invites us to consider both the seasons of life and the issue of gain in a new way. The question of gain is, as we have seen, a mathematical one. It asks us to sum the benefits and subtract the costs to see what the ultimate balance might be.

When we read the poem in 3:1–8 in light of the question about gain, we realize it presents life not just as a series of seasons but as a series of *opposite* seasons: crying and laughing, mourning and dancing, loving and hating, war and peace. If we approach the poem (and, by extension, life itself) as a mathematical equation, asking about its sum, we are forced to conclude that it has a zero-sum balance. With each season matched by its opposite, life cancels itself out. It is as though it never was. It is nothing.

But surely birth and death, uprooting and planting, killing and healing, tearing and building, crying and laughing, mourning and dancing, throwing and gathering, embracing and avoiding, searching and losing, keeping and throwing, tearing and repairing, refraining and speaking, loving and hating, war and peace—is not nothing. It is emphatically *something*. It is human life in all its beauty and horror, in all its hope and despair, in all its joy and pain, bound together by birth and death.

The Sea Is Never Filled

This image calls to mind another poem in which the Gatherer compares the coming and going of human generations to the ongoing cycles of nature:

> A generation goes, and a generation comes,
> but the earth remains as it always has.
> The sun rises, the sun sets;

> it returns panting to the place where it dawns.
> The wind blows to the south,
> goes around to the north;
> around and around blows the wind;
> the wind returns to its rounds again.
> All streams flow to the sea
> but the sea is never full;
> to the place where the rivers flow,
> there they continue to flow. (1:4–7)

If we approach this poem from the perspective of gain, as the Gatherer does in his framing of the poem in 1:3, we must conclude that nature, too, is engaged in furious efforts that accomplish nothing. The sun races, panting across the sky, arriving back at its starting point just in time to rise again. Likewise, the winds whirl about on their courses, from the north to the south, around and around and around. So, too, the rivers pour endlessly into the sea, yet the sea never reaches capacity. Measured in terms of gain, the natural cycles are but furious activity resulting in nothing.

Yet, one would never tell the sun to stop rising. One would never ask the winds to cease their blowing or the rivers to stop their flowing. Without them, all life would perish. The world would be in darkness. The oceans would be barren. One cannot measure the value of natural cycles in terms of gain, as one measures the balance on a balance sheet at the end of a fiscal year. To do so is to misunderstand the value of nature.

So, too, with human life. In the second half of the poem, the Gatherer goes on to say,

All the words are tiring;
no one is able to speak them.[10] The eye isn't satisfied with seeing
neither is the ear filled up by hearing. (1:8)

One can never say all that can be said. One can never see enough to satisfy the desire to see or hear enough to sate the appetite for hearing. Like the sea, we can never be filled.

If we value human existence only in terms of the gain left over at life's end, we must conclude that all of our hearing and seeing and speaking has been pointless. But if, as the Gath-erer suggests, we learn to think in terms of our *share* rather than our ultimate *gain*, we can learn to appreciate each and every word spoken, each and every sight seen, each and every utterance heard as having its own value in its own moment, no matter how brief.

In this way, the Gatherer compares human life to the cycles of nature. As the sun's setting cancels its rising, so our death will cancel our birth. That doesn't mean the journey across the sky counts for nothing.

Reading Ecclesiastes for Today

After a semester of talking with my students about the Gath-erer's views on death, futility, and the unreliability of God, I like to watch their faces when I tell them that Ecclesiastes was one of the texts read at my wedding. The passage we read was Ecclesiastes 9:7–10, which goes like this:

Go, eat your food joyfully and drink your wine happily because God has already accepted what you do. Let your garments always be white; don't run short of oil for your head. Enjoy your life with your dearly loved spouse all the days of your pointless life that God gives you under the sun—all the days of your pointless life!—because that's your part to play in this life and in your hard work under the sun. Whatever you are capable of doing, do with all your might because there's no work, thought, knowledge, or wisdom in the grave, which is where you are headed. (9:7–10)

Typically, my students love the first part of this passage and find it entirely wedding appropriate. The Gatherer says we should eat and drink joyfully and appreciate the gifts God has given us. We should wear clean clothes and take a shower every day. We should spend time with a partner we love, sharing a life together.

"Why didn't you just stop there?" my students inevitably ask. "That's beautiful! Why did you ruin it with all that stuff about pointlessness and death and the grave?"

But it is the second half of the passage that gives it substance. The idea that we could spend our lives all shiny and happy and holding hands is unrealistic. It's a way of denying death, of pretending that there is a happily-ever-after extending endlessly into some fairy-tale future. But life isn't like that. It's full of heartache and loss—and it inevitably ends in death. To pretend that it doesn't is to live in denial, giving power to the very thing we are afraid of.

By naming death in our wedding, and by making Ecclesiastes a part of our story, my spouse and I committed to living and loving each other authentically, knowing that nothing is guaranteed and that all things will come to an end.

And so it is for all of us. Ecclesiastes reminds us to live life simply, cheerfully, and lovingly—not as a way of denying death, but precisely as a way of making meaning in the face of it. Knowing that life is fleeting, knowing that memory is frail, knowing that death is inevitable, enjoy the moments you are given: Love the people you love. Enjoy the work you do. Eat good food and drink good wine. Savor even the stupid little pointless moments, because that is your share in life. You can't live forever.

Notes

1. Sheldon Solomon, Jeff Greenberg, and Tom Pyszczynski, *The Worm at the Core: On the Role of Death in Life* (New York: Random House: 2015), loc. 114, Kindle.

2. Ecclesiastes 1:2 (5x), 14; 2:1, 11, 15, 17, 19, 21, 13, 26; 3:19; 4:4, 7, 8, 16; 5:7, 10; 6:2, 4, 9, 11, 12; 7:6, 15; 8:10, 14 (2x); 9:9 (2x); 11:8, 10; 12:8 (3x). Verse numbers here and elsewhere refer to the CEB versification. The Hebrew versification varies somewhat.

3. See Robert Williamson Jr., "'In the Way of Righteousness is Life': Symbolic Death Transcendence in Proverbs 10–29," *Journal for the Study of the Old Testament* 38, no. 3 (2014): 363–82.

4. See, for example, Proverbs 12:7; 14:1, 11; 17:6.

5. See Proverbs 10:11; 11:30; 13:14.

6. This insight comes from Ruth Fidler, "Qoheleth in the 'House of God': Text and Intertext in Qoh 4:17–5:6 (Eng. 5:1–7)," *Hebrew Studies* 47 (2006): 12.

7. Nyasha Junior (@NyashaJunior), Twitter, January 19, 2015, 4:22 p.m., http://tinyurl.com/y8kxndrc.

8. Solomon, Greenberg, and Pyszczynski, *Worm at the Core*, loc. 246, Kindle.

9. The CEB translates the phrase verbally as "that's what they're allotted in life." However, the Hebrew is a noun, literally "That's their allotment/share in life."

10. I have adapted the CEB translation by including the definite article

("the words"), as in the Hebrew, and supplying the pronoun "them" as the object of "to speak."

5

Esther

Soon after the 2016 United States presidential election cycle, the Southern Poverty Law Center (SPLC), one of the nation's leading civil rights organizations, published a report examining the rise of white nationalism in mainstream American politics.[1] While racial and ethnic hatred have a long history in the United States, the SPLC report showed that ideological extremes that had long been confined to the margins of political discourse were suddenly gaining traction in the mainstream. Former Klan leader David Duke felt emboldened enough to run for the Senate, tweeting that "everything I've been talking about for decades is coming true and the ideas I've fought for have won."[2] Others felt empowered to march through the streets of Charlottesville shouting "Jews will not replace us!"

In October 2017, author Sasha Polakow-Suransky published an opinion piece in the online *New York Times* entitled "White Nationalism Is Destroying the West." She wrote,

Anti-Semitic and xenophobic movements did not disappear from Europe after the liberation of Auschwitz, just as white supremacist groups have lurked beneath the surface of American politics ever since the Emancipation Proclamation. What has changed is that these groups have now been stirred from their slumber by savvy politicians seeking to stoke anger toward immigrants, refugees, and racial minorities for their own benefit. Leaders from Donald Trump to France's Marine Le Pen have validated the worldview of these groups, implicitly or explicitly encouraging them to promote their hateful opinions openly. As a result, ideas that were once marginal have now gone mainstream.[3]

Whatever one's political leanings, the resurgence of white ethnic nationalism in the United States and around the world is deeply troubling. Ethnic minorities, religious minorities, LGBTQI people, and women live in fear of being targeted, both personally and politically.

On its surface, the book of Esther is the rags-to-riches tale of a young Jewish girl who defies all odds to become queen of the great Persian Empire. Yet beneath this fairy-tale appearance, the book confronts us with some of the most fundamental questions about what it means to live courageously in a time in which the ruling authorities are empowering the forces of ethnic hatred against the people.

At its core, the book of Esther tells the story of Jewish resistance to an ethnic cleansing perpetrated by a power-hungry official in the court of a hapless but mercurial king. It tells the story of women resisting the power of ingrained patriarchy and of common people standing up against leaders who sacrifice their well-being in order to glorify themselves. The book of Esther speaks to a time such as ours.

Reading Esther: Setting the Stage

The book of Esther is set in the court of a Persian king it calls Ahasuerus, most likely a reference to the Persian ruler Xerxes, who ruled from 486–465 BCE. While Ahasuerus is thus recognizable as a figure from history, the events portrayed in the book of Esther are almost undoubtedly fictionalized. There is no record of a Jewish queen of Persia, nor of a Persian queen named Esther. The wife of the historical Xerxes was named Amestris, and there is no record of him deposing a previous wife named Vashti.

Rather, the book of Esther should probably be read as a historical novella, set in the court of a historical king but depicting events not as a historical record but as a way of reflecting on the possibilities and perils of being Jewish in the time of Persian rule. Given its lack of references to the Jewish homeland—even to the Jerusalem Temple—the book of Esther seems to have been written by and for Jews living in the diaspora, the descendants of those exiled from Jerusalem during the reign of the Babylonian king Nebuchadnezzar.

The dating of the book of Esther is uncertain, though for obvious reasons it couldn't have been written prior to the reign of Xerxes. The book is usually dated to sometime in the fourth or third centuries BCE.

Exposing the Patriarchy

The book of Esther begins with the story not of Esther but of another woman, named Vashti, who is Esther's predecessor as

Persian queen. By the end of the story, Vashti will have been deposed as queen, but not before exposing the patriarchy that undergirds her husband's rule over the Persian Empire.

The story opens with King Ahasuerus hosting a festival for all the imperial officials. His plan is to "show off the awesome riches of his kingdom and beautiful treasures as mirrors of how very great he was" (1:4). The celebration of Ahasuerus's ego is preposterous in both its size and duration, occupying the entire ruling class of Persia for "six whole months" (1:4). One wonders who was running the empire!

Not satisfied with six months of nonstop partying, Ahasuerus calls for a second feast immediately following the first. This one is a week-long affair for all the locals living in the capital city of Susa. All the men attend the king's party, while the women attend a parallel feast hosted by Queen Vashti (1:5–9).

After a week of heavy drinking, King Ahasuerus calls for Vashti to come before his all-male drinking party wearing the royal crown. The narrator tells us that Vashti "was gorgeous, and he [Ahasuerus] wanted to show off her beauty to the general public and to his important guests" (1:11). For the king, Vashti is another of the objects in his royal treasury, her beauty a testimony to his own ego.

Yet, when the eunuchs summon Vashti, she refuses to come (1:12). Unwilling to be displayed among the king's treasures, Vashti defies the king in this most public of settings, for everyone to see. At the culmination of six months of self-glorification, the king's party ends in his public humiliation.

Angry, the king calls together his trusted advisers to discuss Vashtigate. While he frames his inquiry as a legal issue, it is clear that he plans to carry out a personal vendetta against the woman who has shamed him in public. He asks, "According to the law, what should I do with Queen Vashti since she didn't do what King Ahasuerus ordered her through the eunuchs?" (1:15).

The advisers respond not with relevant penal codes or with meticulous citations of precedential case law. Instead, they express anxiety about how Vashti's act of defiance might empower the other women of the empire—including their own wives—to do the same. One of the advisers, Memucan, says,

> Queen Vashti . . . has done something wrong not just to the king himself. She has also done wrong to all the officials and the peoples in all the provinces of King Ahasuerus. This is the reason: News of what the queen did will reach all women, making them look down on their husbands. They will say, "King Ahasuerus ordered servants to bring Queen Vashti before him, but she refused to come." This very day, the important women of Persia and Media who hear about the queen will tell the royal officials the same thing. There will be no end of put-downs and arguments. (1:16–18)

Memucan's words reveal the extent to which Vashti's defiance has exposed the fragility of the patriarchy, which has until now—like all ideologies—seemed natural and unavoidable.

Women have obeyed their husbands because they didn't

know they had any other choice. But by refusing to obey the king, Vashti has shown that things could be otherwise. If Vashti can refuse the king, other women need not come running at their husbands' commands. They could refuse. Perhaps they could even give commands of their own. And this, the advisers say, simply will not do.

Threatened by the possibility of a new protofeminist consciousness among the women of the empire, engendered by Vashti's previously unthinkable act of defiance, the king's advisers move quickly to enshrine their own power in the kingdom's legal codes. They advise the king, saying,

> Send out a royal order and have it written into the laws of Persia and Media, laws no one can ever change. It should say that Vashti will never again come before King Ahasuerus. It should also say that the king will give her royal place to someone better than she. (1:19)

Once this order has become public, they say, "All women will treat their husbands properly" (1:20). The king issues a decree saying that "each husband should rule over his own house" (1:22).

Of course, the law recommended by the king's advisers is little more than a thinly veiled threat. Just as Vashti was put away by the king for refusing him, so too will the women of the empire be put away by their husbands if they do not obey. As a result, the logic goes, they will be too afraid to try anything similar.

Threatened and exposed, the patriarchy does what the patriarchy always does. If it cannot make itself seem like the natural order of things, it falls back to the next position, entrenching itself in the legal codes or in economic practices or in stereotypes about women in leadership—it uses its power to reinforce its power.

Vashti's Legacy

The text doesn't tell us much about Vashti or her motivations for refusing the king. Perhaps she was tired of being the king's trophy wife, and her refusal was a way of demanding respect from the king and his advisers. She was, after all, the queen. Or perhaps Vashti feared for her safety, wise enough not to trust the intentions of a roomful of men who had been drinking and carousing for a week. Some have speculated that Vashti simply wanted to be left alone, such that the king's "punishment" of deposing her was exactly what she had hoped to achieve.[4]

Yet, we might also read Vashti as attempting to organize a movement, intending exactly the outcome that Ahasuerus's advisers fear—that all the women of the empire would realize that they, too, could refuse. Perhaps Vashti understood that her position as queen provided her a platform to advocate for women who needed the cover of someone more highly placed in order to find their own voices. The king's advisers—not the wisest lot—certainly understood the potential of her action to empower the women of the empire. It's safe to assume she did, too.

If Vashti did indeed hope to inspire a movement, her act of resistance to the patriarchal system at first appears to have been a failure. Her strong, public act of defiance produces a strong, public response from the king's advisers, who reinforce the patriarchal structures of power by enshrining them in the legal code. Yet, even this is a victory of sorts. Ideologies love nothing more than to operate quietly in the background, seeming so "natural" as to be unquestionable. Vashti's act of refusal drags the patriarchal ideology out into the public, raising doubts about whether a woman's unquestioning obedience is really the "natural" way of things. Vashti has forced the patriarchy out of the background and into the legal code where it can be seen, recognized, and challenged. This is a necessary step on the way to the liberation of women.

Further, we really don't know the effect of Vashti's refusal on the women of the empire. The king and his advisers anticipated that women would hear of Vashti and engage in their own acts of resistance and refusal. While no doubt some were cowed back into submission by the king's decree, surely in the vastness of the empire, there were some women who heard of Vashti's example and realized that they, too, could stand up for themselves.

One of those women of the empire who had no doubt heard of Vashti's example was a young Jewish girl named Esther. While Esther never mentions Vashti, she follows in her footsteps—both as the new queen and as a woman who uses her position to resist the abuse of power within the empire. Though Esther exercises her influence quite differently than Vashti, she nonetheless continues Vashti's work of resistance and refusal.

Auditioning a New Queen

Following the story of Vashti, the text jumps forward three years to a time when "King Ahasuerus was less angry" (2:1).[5] That he is only "less angry" even after three years suggests how fragile his kingly ego must be and how prone to fits of rage he is. At this stage, the king's servants convince him it is time to replace Vashti, proposing an empire-wide search for a new queen:

> Let the king have a search made for beautiful young women who haven't yet married. And let the king choose certain people in all the royal provinces to lead the search. Have them bring all the beautiful women together to the fortified part of Susa, to the women's house, to the care of Hegai the king's eunuch in charge of the women so that he might provide beauty treatments for them. Let the young woman who pleases you the most take Vashti's place as queen. (2:2–4)

The servants' plan for finding a new queen indicates that neither they nor King Ahasuerus have learned anything from Vashti's earlier protest. As with Vashti, the women have no agency in the selection process, which is essentially a snatch-and-grab operation. Women don't volunteer for their chance to be queen but are rounded up by the king's officials, apparently with no chance of refusal. Once the women have joined the king on his casting couch, they are to be kept in the harem as secondary wives (2:14). If he has learned anything from his experience with Vashti, it is that he can force women to do anything he wants, backed up by the force and weight of the empire.

It is in this context that we meet Esther, one of the women

gathered for the king's contest (2:5–9). The text introduces her first by her Jewish name, Hadassah (meaning "myrtle"), before switching to her Persian name, Esther (meaning "star"). Her two names serve as a reminder of her dual identities as both a Jew and a member of Persian society. This tension between Esther's Jewishness and her status in Persian society becomes one of the driving forces of the book.

We also learn that Esther has been raised by the other major protagonist of the book, her cousin Mordecai, who adopted her following the death of her parents (2:7). Mordecai is said to be a Benjaminite "from the family line of Shimei and Kish" (5:5), a genealogy that connects Mordecai to Saul, the first king of Israel. Mordecai works as a guard at the King's Gate (2:21–23) and lives "in the fortified part of Susa" (2:5).

The text doesn't tell us how either Esther or Mordecai feels about Esther's selection for the contest. We know only that Mordecai spends his days "pacing back and forth along the wall in front of the women's house to learn how Esther was doing and what they were doing to her" (2:11). That Mordecai has warned Esther not to reveal her Jewish background (2:10) indicates that he has at least some anxiety about her well-being in the king's palace.

For her part, Esther keeps quiet about her ethnic background and entrusts herself to the care of the eunuch Hegai, who takes a particular liking to her. When at last she is called in for her evening audition with King Ahasuerus, Esther, like the other women, is given the opportunity to take anything she wants to the encounter (2:13). Yet Esther takes "nothing except what Hegai the king's eunuch in charge of the women told her" (2:15).

Esther's decision to follow Hegai's advice to the letter, as she has also done with Mordecai's advice to keep her identity a secret, may make her seem like a weak character in comparison to the more self-assured Vashti. In fact, her obedience to the men around her, in addition to her "beautiful figure" (2:7), may help explain how she charms the king, given his continued anger about the previous queen, who had refused him. Yet, Esther's obedience does not need to indicate mindlessness. Rather, as subsequent events reveal, Esther may simply be shrewd enough to discern what advice is to her advantage and agreeable enough to gain the favor of those in power. Indeed, it is precisely Esther's ability to walk this line—to find the advantage in a situation while working within the bounds of expected protocol—that will ultimately save her life and the lives of her people.

When Esther goes in to see the king, taking only those things Hegai recommended, she charms him immediately. In the space of one verse, the narrator reports that Ahasuerus "loved Esther more than all the other women," placing the crown on her head and making her queen "in the place of Vashti" (2:17).

The mention of Vashti draws our attention back to the beginning of the story, inviting a comparison of the two queens. The depiction of a "magnificent, lavish feast" known as the "feast of Esther" likewise parallels Vashti's feast in chapter 1 and reminds us of her refusal. At last, with Esther now in the place of Vashti, Ahasuerus finally achieves his desire of having his queen appear at a banquet before his courtiers.

Saving the King's Life

Following the story of Esther's coronation comes a short notice about Mordecai and Esther saving the life of the Persian king. Two of the king's eunuchs, Bigthan and Teresh, guards stationed at the king's doorway, "became angry with Ahasuerus . . . [and] secretly planned to kill him" (2:21). The text gives us no detail about the motivations of the two eunuchs—only that they were "angry."

What we do know is that Mordecai, who is also a guard stationed at the door of the king's chambers, overhears their plan and reports them to Esther, now the queen, who in turn reports the matter to the proper authorities. After an investigation, the two are found guilty and impaled on pointed poles—a fate that will befall others in the book of Esther, as well.

This brief story, seemingly tangential at this point, becomes a pivotal moment in the plot later on.

Haman's Plot

The main conflict of the book of Esther begins in chapter 3 with the introduction of an imperial official named Haman. A little backstory may help us understand some of the forthcoming conflict between Haman and Mordecai.

Haman is described as "the Agagite," meaning that he is

a descendant of Agag, the Amalekite king executed by the Israelite prophet Samuel in the time of King Saul. According to the story in 1 Samuel 15, God had commanded Saul and the Israelites to attack Agag and the Amalekites, exterminating all of them—"women, men, children and infants, oxen and sheep, camels and donkeys" (1 Samuel 15:3). Saul and the Israelites had carried out that order, massacring all of the Amalekites except for Agag, whose life Saul spared. However, angry that Saul had disobeyed the divine command by sparing Agag, God rejected Saul as king, ultimately replacing him with King David. Agag was then executed by the prophet Samuel (1 Samuel 15:33).

To complicate things further, God's command for the Israelites to kill the Amalekites was itself a response to an even earlier incident in which the Amalekites had attacked the Israelites just as they were escaping out of slavery in Egypt. Exodus 17:8–15 describes how the Amalekites attacked the Israelites at Rephidim, barely two months after the Israelites had escaped from Egypt. After the Israelites had defeated Amalek in a miraculous victory, God swore an oath saying: "I will completely wipe out the memory of Amalek under the sky" (Exodus 17:14). A generation later, as the Israelites were about to enter the promised land, Moses had reminded them about the oath saying, "You must wipe out Amalek's memory from under the heavens. Don't forget this!" (Deuteronomy 25:19).

Thus, while the book of Esther makes no mention of the longstanding blood feud between the Israelites and the

Amalekites, the introduction of Haman the Agagite into the story of Mordecai the Jew is heavily fraught. Their interactions carry the weight of an ethnic hatred extending back more than a millennium to the very earliest days of the Israelite people. That Mordecai and Esther are descendants of Saul—the very king who lost his kingdom by sparing the life of Haman's ancestor Agag—adds even more intrigue to the plot. Had Saul not spared Agag, God may not have rejected him as king. When the time comes to execute Haman, Mordecai and Esther will not make the same mistake.

When we first meet Haman, King Ahasuerus has just promoted him to the position of second-in-command over the empire, above all the other officials. The king has also commanded that all of the workers at the King's Gate should "kneel and bow facedown to Haman" (3:2). While the other guards comply, Mordecai refuses to kneel.

Mordecai's defiance of Haman parallels Vashti's defiance of Ahasuerus in important ways.[6] Both are personal acts of resistance, one person acting alone in defiance of a royal order. However, both are also public acts, bringing shame upon a more powerful ruler, who must respond to restore his honor. Perhaps for this reason, both draw retributions entirely disproportionate to the acts. Ahasuerus banishes Vashti forever and declares an imperial law requiring all women to obey their husbands. Haman, knowing that Mordecai is a Jew (3:4), decides not only to execute Mordecai himself but to exterminate the entire Jewish people. The autocrat does not tolerate defiance.

Before he can carry out his revenge, Haman must convince Ahasuerus to support his plan. Haman approaches the king strategically, accusing the Jews of being a destabilizing force in the empire simply because they have their own laws and customs:

> A certain group of people exist in pockets among the other peoples in all the provinces of your kingdom. Their laws are different from those of everyone else, and they refuse to obey the king's laws. There's no good reason for the king to put up with them any longer. (3:8)

Haman makes what is essentially a law-and-order argument to justify violence against the Jewish ethnic minority—a tactic still employed against minority populations today. He implies that the Jews are lawbreakers because "they refuse to obey the king's laws," but he gives no evidence that this is actually true. He uses the veneer of the law to justify his own personal vendetta against an ethnic minority.

To sweeten the deal, Haman also offers a bribe:

> If the king wishes, let a written order be sent out to destroy them, and I will hand over ten thousand kikkars of silver to those in charge of the king's business. The silver can go into the king's treasuries. (3:9)

The offer of ten thousand kikkars of silver is extravagant. A kikkar weighs approximately 75 pounds, so Haman's offer amounts to about 750,000 pounds of silver. According to one scholar's calculations, that amount would equal about two-thirds of the annual budget of the entire Persian empire.[7] If that calculation is correct, Haman's offer would be like someone offering the president of the United States $2.5 trillion!

Notably, Haman doesn't even mention the name of the people he wants to annihilate; nor does Ahasuerus ask. The accusation of law-breaking and the extravagance of the bribe are quite enough. Ahasuerus gives Haman permission to "do as you like with them" (3:11).

After speaking with Ahasuerus, Haman sends out orders to the entire empire, written in the name of King Ahasuerus and sealed with his ring. The order Haman sends to all the empire commands the people "to wipe out, kill, and destroy all the Jews, both young and old, even women and children" (3:13). Perhaps the threefold repetition of verbs—any one of which would do—reflects the degree of hatred and disgust Haman has for the Jews.

Haman sends out messengers to announce the decree on the thirteenth day of the first month (3:12), which is nearly a year before the genocide is to be carried out on the thirteenth day of the twelfth month, a date chosen by casting lots (3:7). Ironically, Haman's order goes out on the day before Passover, which is celebrated on the fourteenth day of the first month (see Exodus 12:1–6; Leviticus 23:5). Even as Haman plots the destruction of the Jews, his actions unwittingly foreshadow their salvation.

Imagine for a moment the effect of Haman's order on the empire. He has decreed not that the *army* will carry out a genocide against the Jews but that the *people* should seek out and kill their Jewish neighbors. Not only that, but he has declared it ahead of time, so that the whole empire must tremble in fearful anticipation for nearly a year. This is helter-skelter governance.

The text tells us that

> while the king and Haman sat down to have a drink, the city of Susa was in total shock. (3:15)

Haman and Ahasuerus have declared a race war in order to settle a personal vendetta—throwing the entire empire into shock—all while sipping a cocktail.

For a Moment Like This

When the news of Haman's order reaches Mordecai, he responds with traditional Jewish signs of mourning and repentance—tearing his robes, putting on mourning clothes, and putting ashes on his head (4:1). Throughout the empire, the Jews "gave up eating and spent whole days weeping and crying out loudly in pain," as well as lying on the ground "in mourning clothes and ashes" (4:3).

Mordecai, still wearing his mourning clothes, heads into the streets of the city where he stages a public protest, crying out "loudly and bitterly" against the king's decree. Yet Mordecai's protests are not able to reach all the way to the king. He must stop at the King's Gate because "it was against the law for anyone to pass through it wearing mourning clothes" (4:2).

Clearly the king is not interested in public protest. He doesn't want to know of the people's anger and lamentation, so he prohibits them from coming close to him. The isolation of the royal court is so complete that Esther doesn't even seem to have heard of the king's decree until Mordecai sends her a report of "everything that had happened to him" and "a copy of the law made public in Susa concerning the Jews' destruction" (4:7–8).

In a message delivered by the eunuch Hathach, Mordecai orders Esther "to go to the king to seek his kindness and his help for her people" (4:8). Yet things are not so simple. Esther responds:

> There is a single law in a case like this. Any man or woman who comes to the king in the inner courtyard without being called is to be put to death. Only the person to whom the king holds out the gold scepter may live. (4:11)

The king so insulates himself from the imperial *realia* that he doesn't allow his people—not even his own queen—to approach him without the threat of potential death. One does not know whether the king will extend his scepter or have them executed. No sensible person would dare approach the king under those conditions.

Esther's initial refusal to speak to Ahasuerus on behalf of her people prompts Mordecai to respond with what are probably the best-known words from the book of Esther:

> Don't think for one minute that, unlike all the other Jews, you'll come out of this alive simply because you are in the palace. In fact, if you don't speak up at this very important time, relief and rescue will appear for the Jews from another place, but you and your family will die. But who knows? Maybe it was for a moment like this that you came to be part of the royal family. (4:13–14)

Mordecai warns Esther that her privileged position in the royal court can't protect her from the genocide facing her people. Successful assimilation to the culture doesn't ensure protection from evil. Forces of ethnic hatred have a way of redrawing lines that have ostensibly been erased, as the Nazis demonstrated in 1930s Europe. While many Jews had fully integrated into German society, with many no longer considering themselves religiously Jewish, the 1935 Nuremburg Laws redefined the category *Jew* along ethnic lines, declaring that only those of German ancestry could be German citizens. Like the so-called "one-drop rule" in the Jim Crow South, the laws sought an ethnic purity that suddenly excluded many who had thought themselves fully assimilated into the dominant culture. Esther dares not underestimate the threat that ethnic hatred poses to her people.

Lost in the exchange is the fact that it was Mordecai who had created the situation that now imperils their people. One way to understand Mordecai's refusal to bow to Haman is that he was simply being prideful—he should have knelt before Haman and avoided the whole situation. Yet, since the beginning Mordecai seems to have been aware of an anti-Jewish sentiment lurking just beneath the imperial surface. He had warned Esther not to reveal her Jewish identity when she entered the court (2:10, 20). On the promotion of an Amalekite to second-in-command, he had refused to bow (3:1–5). Now he tells Esther that if she tries to hide, her Jewishness will eventually be rooted out (4:13).

It seems that Mordecai has known that ethnic hatred

against the Jews has long seethed throughout the empire, lurking on the fringes and biding its time. Now that one of its own has been promoted to second-in-command, that hatred can move into the center of power. Read this way, Mordecai's refusal to bow to Haman is a way of chasing ethnic hatred into the light, forcing it to admit what it is so it can be defeated. As Vashti's refusal exposed the forces of patriarchy throughout the empire, so Mordecai's refusal exposes anti-Jewish sentiment throughout the empire.

Mordecai's plot is a dangerous one, as he himself doesn't have the power to defeat the ethnic hatred he has called into the light. Only Esther can do that, since only Esther has access to the king. She is now the only hope for her people, and she must act.

Esther hasn't sought this role. She never intended to be in a position to save her people. She is simply someone who recognizes, rather reluctantly in fact, that circumstances have conspired in such a way that she must now do what she can on behalf of her people.

Even so, Mordecai doesn't believe this confluence of events is an accident. He tells Esther that it was "for a moment like this that you came to be part of the royal family" (4:14). He likewise insists that, even if Esther does not act, "relief and rescue will appear for the Jews from another place" (4:14).

Curiously, while Mordecai seems to believe that there is a benevolent force guiding events and ultimately protecting the Jews, neither he nor the book of Esther itself ever refers to this force as "God." While it is certainly reasonable to see

God's hand in the events of Esther, the book would also allow us to think more in terms of a beneficent fate or even the arc of the moral universe. At the very least, the book has a far less personal view of God than many other biblical texts. It has no expectation that God will send a plague, separate a sea, or appear as a pillar of fire. Rather, it emphasizes the very human actions of Mordecai and Esther necessary to save the Jews from destruction.

Emboldened by Mordecai's words, Esther decides to act in resistance to the forces of ethnic hatred taking hold in the empire. Taking charge of the plot for the first time, she orders Mordecai to gather the Jews of Susa for a three-day fast. The purpose of the fast is not to secure the favor of God, as is often the case with fasting, but "to make me brave" (4:15). With the help of her community, Esther summons her courage to save her people: "I will go to the king, and if I am to die, then die I will" (4:16).

Esther's Plan

In the plan that unfolds in the following chapter, Esther demonstrates her astute ability to navigate within an unstable politics of power in order to save her people. Demonstrating a keen understanding of both Ahasuerus and Haman—and the motivations of men like them—Esther bides her time, working within accepted protocols to set the two men against each other, ultimately turning the tables on Haman.

Esther does have an advantage in a palace driven by male egos. Because she is a woman, the powerful men never see her coming. In the patriarchal order of Ahasuerus's empire, the role of a woman is to be beautiful and to be obedient—they have even encoded this in law (1:22). Esther has won the king's hand not only by "having a beautiful figure" and "being lovely to look at" (2:7) but also by carefully doing what she was told by both Hegai (2:15) and Mordecai (2:20). Now taking charge of the fate of her people, Esther uses the men's underestimation of her to great advantage. In doing so, she takes her place in a long line of biblical women who have succeeded in a male-dominated world by outwitting the more powerful men around them: Rebekah, Rachel, Tamar, Shiphrah and Puah, and Rahab, to name but a few.

After three days of fasting, Esther appears in the inner courtyard of the palace wearing her royal clothes (5:1). By doing so, she risks her life, as she has told us of the law that anyone who enters the inner courtyard may be put to death if the king does not extend the royal scepter (4:11). But when the king sees her, he not only extends his scepter but rashly offers her "anything—even half the kingdom" (5:3).

With this offer on the table, a less insightful person than Esther may simply have seized the moment to ask for the king to rescind Haman's order concerning the Jews. Yet, as biblical scholar Sidnie White Crawford observes, that "would not neutralize Haman."[8] Esther knows that the danger to her people lies not only in the specific decree commanding their extermination but also in the man who issued the decree in the first place. Ethnic hatred cannot be defeated merely by the reversal of one policy. It must be rooted out at the source.

In her measured response, Esther asks for the king and Haman to join her for a feast that she has prepared (5:4). As they sit drinking wine together, the king again tells Esther that he will give her anything she asks, even up to half the kingdom (5:6). Yet again, Esther demurs. Instead, she invites the king and Haman to yet another banquet the following day. "Tomorrow," she says, "I will answer the king's questions" (5:8).

Esther's strategy has the desired effect on Haman, who leaves the banquet quite full of himself. He gathers his wife and friends in his home to brag about all his successes, including how "the king had honored him by promoting him over the officials and high royal workers" (5:11). Curiously, he also boasts to them about "his great wealth and many sons"—as if his wife and friends didn't already know about them! This is not a man celebrating his success with his friends and family. This is a man who craves adulation.

For Haman, Esther's invitation is the crowning glory of his rise to prominence in the kingdom. He tells his friends,

> Queen Esther has invited no one else but me to join the king for food and drinks that she has prepared. In fact, I've been called to join the king at her place tomorrow! (5:12)

Haman is on top of the world—at the zenith of his power—seemingly unstoppable.

And yet he cannot shake his irritation that one man in all the empire, Mordecai, doesn't respect and admire him. Leaving Esther's banquet, he had seen Mordecai at the King's Gate, and Mordecai had "neither stood up nor seemed the least bit nervous around him" (5:9). This slight, Haman tells his friends, ruins everything else. "All this loses its meaning every time I see Mordecai the Jew sitting at the King's Gate," he says (5:13).

To placate him, Haman's wife Zeresh and his friends propose a plan:

> Have people prepare a pointed pole seventy-five-feet high. In the morning, tell the king to have Mordecai impaled on it. Then you can go with the king to the feast in a happy mood. (5:14)

Clearly, erecting a seventy-five-foot stake is a fairly inefficient means of executing one's enemies. Rather, such a spectacle would send a message to the entire city that Haman is not to be disrespected or trifled with. Only someone with disproportionate power and resources could afford to create such an over-the-top display. As Ahasuerus has demonstrated with his six-month banquet, powerful men don't do anything small—and this execution would be no exception. Simultaneously demonstrating Haman's power and displaying Mordecai's shame would surely put Haman in a good mood for dinner.

Notably, the text attributes the plan to "his wife Zeresh and all his friends" (5:14), focusing on Zeresh as the main proponent of the plan. Whatever else we may say about the book of Esther, it elevates the role of female characters in the plot more than any other biblical book except perhaps Ruth. While the men are in the positions of institutional power in this text, it is the women who are driving the action.

Ironic Reversal

At this point, the narrative shifts from the story of Esther's plan and focuses for a moment on the king, who is restless in his bed chamber (6:1). Unable to sleep, he calls for the court records to be read to him. As they are read, they come to the record about the time Mordecai saved the king's life by reporting a plot against him, as was earlier told in 2:21–23. Ahasuerus asks what has ever been done to honor Mordecai, to which his servants reply "Nothing" (6:3).

It is an unexpected twist that Mordecai's act of loyalty, which occurred five years earlier, should resurface at this propitious moment.[9] That these particular records should happen to be read on this particular night, just when Haman is plotting Mordecai's death, can't be coincidence. Whether or not we see God's hand here, the text does seem to be making a point about the moral nature of the world: eventually people do get what they deserve. Mordecai, who saved the king's life, has up until now received nothing in return, but now the king will honor him. By the same token, the wicked Haman has so far prospered, rising to the second position in the empire despite his genocidal tendencies. Will he not also get what he deserves? Of course he will.

In a beautifully ironic passage, Haman enters the courtyard "to tell the king to impale Mordecai on the pole that he had set up for him" (6:4) at the very moment that the king has decided to reward Mordecai. When the king asks, "What should be done for the man whom the king really wants to honor?" (6:6), Haman thinks that the king must want to honor him—how could he not after Esther had flattered him so? He replies:

> Here's what should be done for the man the king really wants to honor. Have servants bring out a royal robe that the king himself has worn and a horse on which the king himself has ridden. It should have a royal crest on its head. Then hand over the robe and the horse to another man, one of the king's officials. Have him personally robe the man whom the king really wants to honor and lead him on the horse through the city square. As he goes, have him shout, "This is what the king does for the man he really wants to honor!" (6:7–9)

The request is shocking in its forwardness. Haman declares the honoree should wear clothes the king has worn and ride a horse the king has ridden, complete with the royal crest on its head. The line between wishing to be *honored* by the king and wishing to *be* the king is thin, and Haman walks it rather tightly.

As a result, the reversal that follows proves enormously satisfying for the reader. The king declares that Haman should do everything he has just said—which of course Haman had intended to be done in honor of himself—for his hated enemy Mordecai. We can't help but laugh at the image of Mordecai processing through the city dressed as a king and riding the king's horse, while Haman walks along beside shouting, "This is what the king does for the man he really wants to honor!" The shame Haman feels must be palpable—he goes home quite literally wearing a bag over his head (6:12).

Esther Defeats Haman

Just as Haman arrives home, the eunuchs come to escort him to his final banquet with Esther and the king. As the three drink wine together, the king asks Esther for the third time,

> What is your wish Queen Esther? I'll give it to you. And what do you want? I'll do anything—even give you half the kingdom. (7:2)

While this time Esther does respond, she yet again approaches her request cautiously, calculating how to elicit the desired response from the king. Esther parses the king's words carefully, recognizing that he has in fact opened the door for not one but two requests, first saying "What is your wish?" (*mah she'elatekh*) and then "What do you want?" (*mah baqashatekh*). Esther in turn responds by making two requests:

> If it please the king, and if the king wishes, give me my life—that's my wish—and the lives of my people too. That's my desire. (7:3)

She mirrors the king's language, asking for her own life "as my wish" (*bi-she'elati*) and the life of her people "as my desire" (*be-baqashati*).

As the king has no doubt expected Esther to ask for something of material value—up to half the kingdom he has said—her plea for her life and the life of her people must strike an emotional chord with him, particularly in light of the hospitality she has shown him during the previous two days. Yet Esther couches her request not in emotional terms but in economic ones. She continues,

> We have been sold—I and my people—to be wiped out, killed, and destroyed. If we simply had been sold as male and female slaves, I would have said nothing. But no enemy can compensate the king for this kind of damage. (7:4)

Even when pleading for her life, Esther places the king's needs first, appealing not to his emotions but to his profit margins. She would be fine to be sold into slavery, she says, where she and her people could continue to serve the king's interests. But to be wiped out makes no economic sense. How can they serve the king when they are dead?

Notably, Esther hasn't mentioned Haman at all. She could have accused him directly, but such an accusation would likely raise defensiveness in the king, whose instinct would be to defend his second-in-command. Astutely, Esther refrains from naming Haman, allowing the king to pass judgment on an unnamed perpetrator. He cries,

> Who is this person, and where is he? Who would do such a thing? (7:5)

Esther yet again responds carefully, saying "A man who hates, an enemy!" raising the king's hackles even further, before finally declaring, "This wicked Haman!" (7:6).

Esther's masterful plan finally reaches its culmination with the accusation against Haman. It has taken two days of patient indirection, but by the time Esther finally names Haman, his fate is sealed. As the king storms out of the room, Haman begs Esther for his life. Yet even this pleading backfires for Haman, as the king, returning to the room, mistakenly thinks Haman is molesting his wife (7:8).

One of the eunuchs, Harbona, now casually reminds the king that Haman himself has set up a giant stake upon which to impale his enemy Mordecai. In a last dramatic act of reversal, the king commands "Impale him upon it!" (7:9). Haman's life thus ends in shameful display "on the very pole that he set up for Mordecai" (7:10). The dramatic image communicates the opposite of what Haman intended: anyone who threatens Mordecai and the Jews will be put to shame.

Competing Genocides

With Haman's death, the narrator tells us, "the king's anger went away" (7:10). Once he has given Esther all of Haman's possessions (8:1) and placed Haman's royal ring on Mordecai's finger (8:2), Ahasuerus seems satisfied that the crisis has been resolved. Yet Haman himself was only a small part of the problem, as his order to exterminate all the Jews of Persia yet remains in effect. Ahasuerus seems either to have forgotten this crucial point or not to have really cared about it in the first place. Driven by his emotions and focused on immediate results, Ahasuerus often seems oblivious to the more complex policy issues at hand.

Esther thus finds herself once again taking her life into her own hands, bowing yet again before the king and begging him to treat her kindly. When the king again holds the scepter to her, Esther must repeat her earlier request for him to save her people:

> If the king wishes, and if I please him—that is, if the idea seems right to the king, and if he still sees me as a good person—then

have people write something to call back the order—the order
that put into effect the plan of Haman, Hammedatha the
Agagite's son, that he wrote to destroy the Jews in all the royal
provinces. (8:5)

It seems Esther can't simply appeal to genocide as an inherent
evil that should be stopped. Rather, she appeals again to the
king's personal preferences, asking him to act "if the king
wishes," "if I please him," and "if he still sees me as a good
person" (8:5). The king can't be expected to do what is right
but only to act out of his own personal, emotional attachment
to events.

Nor can the king be bothered to actually handle policy
matters himself. In the incident with Vashti, he had relied on
his advisers to issue the new law about obedience (1:21–22).
So, too, when Haman wished to issue an order to destroy the
Jews, the king had let Haman handle the details: "Both the
people and the money are under your power. Do as you like
with them" (3:11). Now he instructs Esther and Mordecai to
"write to the Jews whatever you like in the name of the king"
(8:8).

Noting that these events take place in the third month
of the year (8:9) and Haman's attack was scheduled for the
twelfth month (3:7), it should have been possible simply to
call the whole thing off. Yet the king reminds them that
"anything written in the name of the king and sealed with the
king's royal ring can't be called back" (8:8). As a result, and as
strange as it seems, Esther and Mordecai can't simply cancel
Haman's ethnic cleansing.

Given the circumstances, Esther and Mordecai issue the most reasonable edict possible. The narrator reports,

The order allowed Jews in each town to join together and defend their lives. The Jews were free to wipe out, kill, and destroy every army of any people and province that attacked them, along with their women and children. They could also take and keep anything their attackers owned. (8:11)

The proclamation gives permission only for the Jews to defend themselves against anyone who tries to kill them. While it does allow that the Jews can "keep anything their attackers owned," the later report about the attacks indicates that "the Jews didn't lay a hand on anything their enemies owned" (9:10, 16). The Jews act purely in self-defense, eliminating only the threat to their own existence and refusing to profit from their victory even though their enemies would gladly have looted them were the situation reversed (3:13).

When the day finally arrives, the texts reports,

On the very day that the enemies of the Jews had hoped to overpower them, the tables were turned against them. The Jews overpowered their enemies instead. (9:1)

The Jews defeat everyone who attacks them, killing seventy-five thousand people throughout the provinces of the empire (9:16) as well as five hundred people plus the ten sons of Haman in the fortified part of Susa (9:6–7).

There is understandably a triumphant tone to these passages in Esther, as the Jews have won a great victory over the enemies who tried killed them. Yet there is tragedy here as well. To begin, the narrator reports,

> All the leaders of the provinces, rulers, governors, and those in charge of the king's business helped the Jews because they were afraid of Mordecai. Because Mordecai was very important in the palace, news about him was sweeping through the provinces. Indeed, Mordecai was becoming more and more important every day. (9:3–4)

As is so often the case, the rulers and officials of the kingdom—the ones who declare the wars—suffer the least from its effects. Because they know the inner workings of the government, they know that Mordecai has risen to power, and they are able to switch sides at the last moment. The common people who lack this insider information are the ones left to the slaughter.

We might respond that those who were killed nonetheless deserved their fate, as they are the ones who had taken up arms to kill the Jews in their communities. While this may be true, we should also remember that the people thought they were responding to a direct order from Ahasuerus, since Haman had written his edict in the king's name and sealed it with the king's ring. No doubt there were people who attacked their Jewish neighbors not because of their own hatred but because they feared the reprisals of the king. They had, after all, seen what happened to Vashti. Ruling through fear erodes the moral foundations of the people, creating an environment in which good people do awful things to each other.

Finally, it seems that the government officials help the Jews not because they are friends of the Jews, or even because they disapprove of Haman's genocidal edict, but because "they were afraid of Mordecai." These are the same men who would have supported Haman's genocide had he still been in power. As a result, the massacre of those who attacked the Jews may have relieved the immediate danger, but it has not eliminated the root of the problem. While ethnic hatred may go underground, until there is true racial understanding born out of love and not fear, it always has the potential to reemerge.

After a second day of fighting, in which the Jews kill an additional three hundred residents of Susa and impale the (already dead) sons of Haman on pointed poles like their father (9:13–15), the killing ends. The text proclaims rather optimistically,

> [The Jews] put to rest the troubles with their enemies and killed those who hated them. (9:16)

Yet, recalling that the history of the fighting between the Jews and Amalekites extends back more than a millennium to the exodus, one doubts whether this latest purging of enemies will accomplish anything more than the previous ones. As subsequent history has demonstrated, ethnic hatred remains a perpetual human problem, directed repeatedly against the Jews and other ethnic groups even in our own time. The purging of one's enemies does not "put to rest the troubles" that persist among us but only reinforces the cycle of violence, now against the Israelites, now against the Amalekites, now against the Israelites, and so on. An ethnic nationalism that seeks to eradicate difference cannot be the answer.

Reading Esther Today

In its original writing, and in its long liturgical use in the Jewish tradition, the book of Esther is a call to resistance against anti-Semitism and a celebration of the resilience of the Jewish people against all who would do them harm. That core message of the book continues to resonate today—whether in the synagogue, in the church, or in society at large—that we must root out anti-Semitism in all its forms and celebrate God's faithfulness to the Jewish people in all times and places.

Yet, the significance of the book for today ripples out from that central message, calling all of us to acts of resistance not only against anti-Semitism but also against all forms of systemic oppression affecting those located outside systems of power. It calls us to resistance against misogyny, against racial oppression, against religious bigotry, against homophobia, against ethnic nationalism—against all forms of power, public and hidden, that privilege some at the expense of the full humanity of others.

Like Esther, Mordecai, and Vashti, we are called to resist in different ways depending on circumstance and opportunity. Some of us may resist like Vashti, who grew tired of being treated like an object and responded with a "No!" Using her privileged position as queen, she sought to create space for other, more vulnerable women to engage in their own acts of refusal, risking her position in the hope of helping someone else improve theirs.

Some of us may resist like Mordecai, who used his act of

refusal to draw ethnic hatred out of the shadows and into the light of day where it could be exposed and recognized. Then, taking to the streets, he made a spectacle until he drew the attention of those in power.

Some of us may resist like Esther, who shrewdly negotiated the halls of power to save the lives of her people. She resisted by studiously following royal protocols and speaking the language of power, winning the king to her side.

But if we are to defeat the powers of hatred emboldened among us, we must all resist. Whoever we are, wherever we are—perhaps our lives have been preparing us for such a time as this.

Notes

1. Ryan Lenz and Booth Gunter, "100 Days in Trump's America: White Nationalists and Their Agenda Infiltrate the Mainstream," Southern Poverty Law Center, April 27, 2017, http://tinyurl.com/y7bm73qr.

2. David Duke (@DrDavidDuke), Twitter, January 31, 2017, 8:52 p.m., http://tinyurl.com/y7wtmk5k.

3. Sasha Polakow-Suransky, "White Nationalism Is Destroying the West," *New York Times*, October 12, 2017, http://tinyurl.com/y8mjnnlr.

4. Sidnie White Crawford, "Esther," in *Women's Bible Commentary*, ed. Carol A. Newsom, Sharon H. Ringe, and Jacqueline E. Lapsley, 3rd ed. (Louisville: Westminster John Knox, 2012), loc. 6988, Kindle.

5. According to Esther 1:3, the Vashti scene is set in the third year of Ahasuerus's reign. Esther is said to meet the king in the seventh year of his reign (2:16) following a year in preparation (2:12), which must then have begun in his sixth year.

6. See Jon D. Levenson, *Esther: A Commentary*, The Old Testament

Library (Louisville: Westminster John Knox, 1997), loc. 1831, Kindle.

7. Lewis Bayles Paton, *A Critical and Exegetical Commentary on the Book of Esther*, International Critical Commentary 13 (Edinburgh: T&T Clark, 1908), 205, cited in Levenson, *Esther*, note 123, Kindle. See Herodotus, *Histories*, 3.95.

8. Crawford, "Esther," loc. 7039, Kindle.

9. The original incident takes place in the seventh year of Ahasuerus (2:16), while the conflicts with Haman occur in his twelfth year (3:7).

A Closing Word

At Mercy Community Church of Little Rock, we like to say that the purpose of Bible study is to help us all think more deeply about the Bible, the world, and our lives. We do our Bible study conversationally, so that everyone has a chance to offer their interpretations to the community. We don't care much about always agreeing with each other, but we do practice trying to understand each other. We try to let every voice matter. What binds us together is not the conclusion of the Bible study but the process of studying the Bible.

Interacting through the pages of a book is obviously a different process, but I hope some of the same principles may apply. My purpose here hasn't been to convince you that my interpretation of these texts is the "right" one or that you should reach the same conclusions about the relationship of the text and the world that I have reached. Rather, I offer these readings of the Five Scrolls as a starting point for conversation. If we were at Mercy Community Church, I would pause now and say, "What do you think about that?" Our interpretations are richer when we read together.

Since I can't be there to talk over these ideas with you (unless you invite me to visit!), I hope that you'll continue the conversation in other ways. I hope you'll go back and read the biblical texts for yourself to see what I've missed. I hope you'll get together with others to wrestle with what the Bible has to say about sex and sexuality, about immigration, about protest, about death and dying, and about ethnic nationalism. I hope you'll dig through the rest of the Bible to see what surprising things it might say about other issues that you're struggling with, about the nature of God, and about what it means to be human.

In whatever is your way, I hope you'll continue to engage. Let's recover the Five Scrolls for today.

For Further Reading

General Works

Alter, Robert. *Strong as Death Is Love: The Song of Songs, Ruth, Esther, Jonah, and Daniel: A Translation with Commentary*. New York: W. W. Norton, 2015.

Edsell, Thomas B. "Forecasting Havoc for Orlando." *The Washington Post*, June 10, 1998. http://tinyurl.com/y6uvws223.

Lazard, Joshua L. "A Theology of Anger: Forgiveness for White Supremacy Derails Action and Alienates Young Black Activists." Religion Dispatches, July 6, 2015. http://tinyurl.com/y8sp6ndw.

Lenz, Ryan, and Booth Gunter. "100 Days in Trump's America: White Nationalists and Their Agenda Infiltrate the Mainstream." Southern Poverty Law Center, April 27, 2017. http://tiny url.com/y7bm73qr.

Marrero, Pilar. *Killing the American Dream: How Anti-Immigration Extremists Are Destroying the Nation*. New York: Palgrave Macmillan, 2012.

Polakow-Suransky, Sasha. "White Nationalism Is Destroying the West." *New York Times*, October 12, 2017. http://tinyurl.com/y8mjnnlr.

Solomon, Sheldon, Jeff Greenberg, and Tom Pyszczynski. *The Worm at the Core: On the Role of Death in Life*. New York: Random House, 2015.

Chapter 1: Song of Songs

Alexander, Philip S. *The Targum of Canticles*. Aramaic Bible 17A. Collegeville, MN: Liturgical, 2003.

Bloch, Ariel, and Chana Bloch. *The Song of Songs: A New Translation*. Berkeley: University of California Press, 1995.

Brenner, Athalya, and Carole R. Fontaine, eds. *The Song of Songs: A Feminist Companion to the Bible (Second Series)*. Sheffield: Sheffield Academic, 2000.

Exum, J. Cheryl. *Song of Songs: A Commentary*. The Old Testament Library. Louisville: Westminster John Knox, 2005.

Fishbane, Michael A. *Song of Songs: The Traditional Hebrew Text with the New JPS Translation*. JPS Bible Commentary. Philadelphia: Jewish Publication Society, 2015.

King, Christopher. "Song of Songs." In *The Queer Bible Commentary*, edited by Deryn Guest. London: SCM, 2006.

Weems, Renita J. "The Song of Songs: Introduction, Commentary, and Reflections." In vol. 5 of *The New Interpreter's Bible*, edited by Leander E. Keck and Richard J. Clifford, 361–434. Nashville: Abingdon, 1997.

Chapter 2: Ruth

Gafney, Wil. "Ruth." In *The Africana Bible: Reading Israel's Scriptures from Africa and the African Diaspora*, edited by Hugh R. Page Jr., 249–54. Minneapolis: Fortress Press, 2010.

Lee, Eunny P. "Ruth." In *Women's Bible Commentary*, edited by Carol A. Newsom, Sharon H. Ringe, and Jacqueline E. Lapsley. 3rd ed. Louisville: Westminster John Knox, 2012.

Linafelt, Tod. *Ruth*. Berit Olam: Studies in Hebrew Narrative and Poetry. Collegeville, MN: Liturgical, 1999.

Nielsen, Kirsten. *Ruth: A Commentary*. The Old Testament Library. Louisville: Westminster John Knox, 1997.

Norton, Yolanda. "Silenced Struggles for Survival: Finding Life in Death in the Book of Ruth." In *I Found God in Me: A Womanist Biblical Hermeneutics Reader*, edited by Mitzi J. Smith. Eugene, OR: Cascade, 2015.

Sasson, Jack M. "Ruth." In *The Literary Guide to the Bible*, edited by Robert Alter and Frank Kermode, 320–28. Cambridge, MA: Belknap Press of Harvard University Press, 1987.

Sasson, Jack M. *Ruth: A New Translation with a Philological Commentary and a Formalist-Folklorist Interpretation*. Baltimore: Johns Hopkins University Press, 1979.

West, Mona. "Ruth." In *The Queer Bible Commentary*, edited by Deryn Guest. London: SCM, 2006.

Yee, Gale. "'She Stood in Tears amid the Alien Corn': Ruth, The Perpetual Foreigner and Model Minority." In *They Were All Together in One Place? Toward Minority Biblical Criticism*, edited by Randall C. Bailey, Tat-Siong Benny Liew, and Fernando F. Segovia, 119–40. Atlanta: Society of Biblical Literature, 2009.

Chapter 3: Lamentations

Bailey, Wilma Ann. *Lamentations*. Believer's Church Bible Commentary. Harrisonburg, VA: Herald, 2015.

Berlin, Adele. *Lamentations*. The Old Testament Library. Louisville: Westminster John Knox, 2002.

Dobbs-Allsopp, F. W. *Lamentations*. Interpretation Bible Commentary. Louisville: John Knox, 2002.

Guest, Deryn. "Lamentations." In *The Queer Bible Commentary*, edited by Deryn Guest. London: SCM, 2006.

Lanahan, William F. "The Speaking Voice in the Book of Lamentations." *Journal of Biblical Literature* 93, no. 1 (1974): 41–49.

O'Connor, Kathleen M. *Lamentations and the Tears of the World*. Maryknoll, NY: Orbis, 2002.

Parry, Robin A. *Lamentations*. Two Horizons Old Testament Commentary. Grand Rapids: Eerdmans, 2010.

Slavitt, David R. *The Book of Lamentations: A Meditation and Translation*. Baltimore, MD: Johns Hopkins University Press, 2001.

Chapter 4: Ecclesiastes

Brown, William P. *Ecclesiastes*. Interpretation Bible Commentary. Louisville: Westminster John Knox, 2000.

Crenshaw, James L. *Ecclesiastes: A Commentary*. The Old Testament Library. Philadelphia: Westminster, 1987.

Fox, Michael V. *A Time to Tear Down and a Time to Build Up: A Rereading of Ecclesiastes*. Grand Rapids: Eerdmans, 1999.

Hopkins, Jamal-Dominique. "Ecclesiastes." In *The Africana Bible: Reading Israel's Scriptures from Africa and the African Diaspora*, edited by Hugh R. Page Jr., 260–65. Minneapolis: Fortress Press, 2010.

Koosed, Jennifer L. "Ecclesiastes." In *Women's Bible Commentary*, edited by Carol A. Newsom, Sharon H. Ringe, and Jacqueline E. Lapsley. 3rd ed. Louisville: Westminster John Knox, 2012.

Pauw, Amy Plantinga. *Proverbs and Ecclesiastes*. Belief. Louisville: Westminster John Knox, 2011.

Tamez, Elsa. *When the Horizons Close: Rereading Ecclesiastes.* Translated by Margaret Wilde. Eugene, OR: Wipf & Stock, 2006.

Towner, W. Sibley. "Ecclesiastes." In vol. 5 of *The New Interpreters Bible*, edited by Leander E. Keck and Richard J. Clifford, 265–360. Nashville: Abingdon, 1997.

Chapter 5: Esther

Beal, Timothy K. *Esther.* Berit Olam: Studies in Hebrew Narrative and Poetry. Collegeville, MN: Liturgical, 1999.

Bechtel, Carol M. *Esther.* Interpretation Bible Commentary. Louisville: John Knox, 2002.

Berlin, Adele. *Esther: The Traditional Hebrew Text with the New JPS Translation.* JPS Bible Commentary. Philadelphia: Jewish Publication Society, 2001.

Crawford, Sidnie White. "Esther." In *Women's Bible Commentary*, edited by Carol A. Newsom, Sharon H. Ringe, and Jacqueline E. Lapsley. 3rd ed. Louisville: Westminster John Knox, 2012.

Day, Linda. *Esther.* Abingdon Old Testament Commentaries. Nashville: Abingdon, 2005.

Levenson, Jon D. *Esther: A Commentary.* The Old Testament Library. Louisville: Westminster John Knox, 1997.

Paton, Lewis Bayles. *A Critical and Exegetical Commentary on the Book of Esther.* International Critical Commentary 13. Edinburgh: T&T Clark, 1908.

West, Mona. "Esther." In *The Queer Bible Commentary*, edited by Deryn Guest. London: SCM, 2006.